which?
essential guides

CV AND
INTERVIEW
HANDBOOK

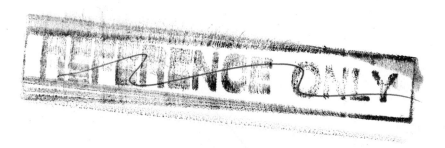

" My greatest frustration is when I see candidates fail because they have sold themselves short. It is easy to avoid this. If you are going to succeed in a highly competitive market, all you need to do is stick to some simple golden rules. "

Sue Tumelty

About the author

Sue Tumelty is the founder and Managing Director of The HR Dept (www.hrdept.co.uk), an Investors in People-awarded company that provides practical human resources support and advice to businesses throughout the UK. During her long career as a senior HR executive, she has been responsible for hiring thousands of people. She is a Chartered Member of the Chartered Institute of Personnel and Development (CIPD) and is qualified with the British Psychological Society, Myers Briggs and Psytech to set and interpret a wide range of psychometric tests.

CV AND INTERVIEW HANDBOOK

SUE TUMELTY

Which? Books are commissioned and published by Which? Ltd,
2 Marylebone Road, London NW1 4DF
Head of Which? Books: Angela Newton
Project management for Which? Books: Claudia Dyer
Email: books@which.co.uk

Distributed by Littlehampton Book Services Ltd, Faraday Close, Durrington, Worthing,
West Sussex BN13 3RB

British Library Cataloguing in Publication Data
A catalogue record for this book is available from the British Library

ISBN 978 1 84490 047 3

1 3 5 7 9 10 8 6 4 2

Author's acknowledgements
Big thanks to all of The HR Dept's wonderful staff, especially Sally McAndrew, our recruitment
specialist, for all her invaluable input, and Tom Doherty who recently gained recognition in the
Bristol Evening Post Recruitment Awards. Thanks also to our writer, Victoria Walker, who
continues to help us with our ongoing mission to find round pegs for round holes.

Edited by: Emma Callery
Designed by: Bob Vickers
Index by: Lynda Swindells
Cover photographs by: Alamy (left); iStock (right)
Printed and bound by VivaPress, Barcelona, Spain

Arctic Volume White is an elemental chlorine free paper produced at Arctic Paper
Hafrestroms AB in Åsensbruk, Sweden, using timber from sustainably managed forests.
The mill is ISO14001 and EMAS certified, and has PEFC and FSC certified Chain of Custody.

For a full list of Which? Books, please call 01903 828557, access our website at
www.which.co.uk, or write to Littlehampton Book Services. For other enquiries call
0800 252 100.

Contents

Introduction

If you want some money, get a job. It's easy, right? Well it may be if you are content to do any old thing, but getting the right job for you is a different matter. First you've got to find one. But what do you do if the one you want is part of the silent majority that are never advertised? Then you've got to try to get an interview.

Think about it. Some jobs, such as graduate trainee schemes offered by some of the big name firms, regularly receive thousands of applications for just a handful of places. That adds up to an awful lot of people who fail, many of whom will have endured a battery of back-to-back tests on everything from their brains to their personality before being rejected. You may be a super smart, self-motivated team player, but if you crack up in your interview, you're out. Job-hunting is not all about failure, however, some people actually do extremely well in the recruitment process. The answer is knowing how to succeed and that is where we come in.

“ You may be super smart and a self-motivated team player, but you have to know how to succeed at job-hunting or you will be out. ”

FIRST JOBS

If you are applying for your first job, you have probably just left school, college or university. Searching for your first job can seem like a daunting prospect. You may be asking yourself why anyone would want to employ you, after all you have no experience and no track record? How could any employer possibly pick you out from all of the other, virtually identical, fellow graduates? You have a point. But it is pretty pessimistic. The fact is that you are in a wonderful position, one that you will never be in again. You are about to embark on your working life and there are many opportunities ahead of you. The trick is getting there and that requires a bit of inside knowledge and some canny preparation.

There are drawbacks, of course. You may need to work your way up to the position you aspire to. But everybody has to start somewhere. This often means the bottom rung of the career ladder and

Whatever your status in the job market, you will find more information concerning what's out there for you in the job market on pages 12–32.

may not quite be the job you imagine yourself doing. Don't let this put you off. Look beyond the immediate situation and work out potential routes to take you where you want to be. It is possible that you will need to work in several different positions, over a number of years, before you secure the job of your dreams. And don't be intimidated by more senior colleagues or potential colleagues. Remember that they had to start somewhere too. Experienced headteachers will have once been newly qualified and looking for their first school. Senior company directors could have begun their careers as graduate trainees. TV presenters may have got their first taste of working in television as runners for production companies.

RETURNING FROM A CAREER BREAK

You may be searching for a new position after having taken a career break to focus on looking after your children, or elderly or disabled relatives. But where do you start? Are you ready for online psychometric testing? Will you be able to cope with the changes that have probably taken place in your chosen industry since you last did it? Advances in computing or other technology can leave many people confused or worried that they are unable to carry on where they left off. Many people feel a lack of confidence and question whether they will remember how to do the basics, especially if it has been several years since they last worked. If this describes you, try to stop worrying. You are not the only one who is new to the latest recruitment practices. Gen up on what's what and concentrate on the qualities that you can bring to the marketplace.

For many people, returning to work signals the end of a period of ill health. This could further help your recovery as many studies have shown that unemployment can have a detrimental effect on our health and general wellbeing. However, you may not be quite ready to work full-time or go back to a position similar to where you left off. Think carefully about how you feel. Talk it through with your health worker or doctor. Perhaps you could start off gently, working part-time, temping or completing some voluntary work as you test the water and see how you feel. Starting back at work in this way may also help your confidence and social skills, giving you a strong grounding for a more demanding role later on.

If you are looking for work after a prison sentence, it will be tough. Even if you have an amazing CV, some employers may harbour prejudices against you. However, it is not all bad and someone out there will give you a job. You just need to know how to get it and once you have secured your first one, everything will just get easier.

❝ After a career break, many people lack confidence and wonder if they will remember how to do the basics in a workplace. ❞

MOVING ON

If you get up in the morning dreading going to work, you are in the wrong job and it is time to move on. But hating your job is only one of the reasons there may be for needing a change. Perhaps you want to further your career or increase your salary but your present employer has no promotion opportunities on offer. You may wish to make changes to your life. This might be a lifestyle decision, downshifting your work with a job that makes fewer demands on your time. Of course, the reverse may also be true. You may seek a job that is more demanding or stimulating.

You may also need to get a new job for reasons outside of your immediate control. Your partner or spouse may be relocated beyond reasonable commuting distance for your job, for example.

❝ Draw up a list of the things you want from a job. These could include stimulation, social interaction or maybe flexibility. ❞

JOB-HUNTING

The first stage of your search will require you to think about what you want from a job. This does not need to be an intense period of self-analysis, but it does require you to think about what is important to you. Draw up a list. Things will be much clearer to you if you write them down. You might want a job that is intellectually stimulating or socially rewarding, or you might prefer one that you can forget about every evening as you walk through the gates at five o'clock. You may find a job where your potential employer promotes flexible working practices, but if the mere thought of a colleague leaving early to watch their child's school play makes your blood boil, this job might not be the best one for you. It will also save you a lot of time if you can define what you don't want before you start applying; in that way you can avoid applying for an unsuitable job in the first place.

Different employers use varying techniques for finding and choosing a new employee. Larger organisations may use a human resources (HR) department to complete the process, adding the relevant manager to the final interview stage. Some employers prefer to outsource the whole procedure to a specialist recruitment or HR agency.

 Despite the growth of technology for both advertising and applying for jobs, recruitment agencies remain of key importance. Their role is explained in Chapter 6 on pages 137–46.

Researching and applying for a job

The journey to starting a new (or your first) job can take various directions.
Follow the path below for an overview of the contents of this book.

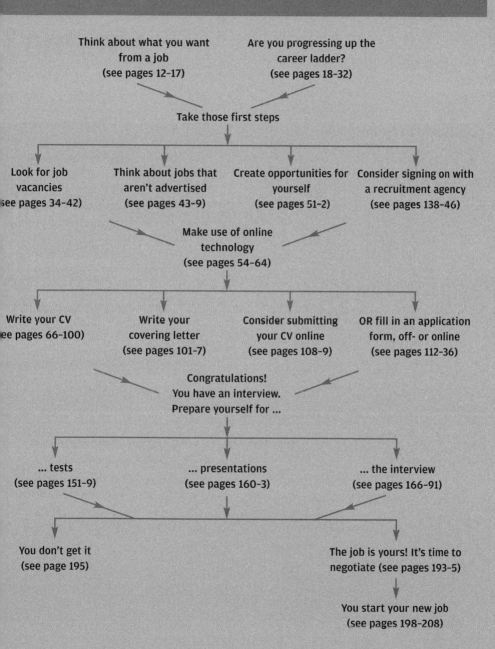

Think about what you want
from a job
(see pages 12–17)

Are you progressing up the
career ladder?
(see pages 18–32)

Take those first steps

Look for job
vacancies
(see pages 34–42)

Think about jobs that
aren't advertised
(see pages 43–9)

Create opportunities for
yourself
(see pages 51–2)

Consider signing on with
a recruitment agency
(see pages 138–46)

Make use of online
technology
(see pages 54–64)

Write your CV
(see pages 66–100)

Write your
covering letter
(see pages 101–7)

Consider submitting
your CV online
(see pages 108–9)

OR fill in an application
form, off- or online
(see pages 112–36)

Congratulations!
You have an interview.
Prepare yourself for ...

... tests
(see pages 151–9)

... presentations
(see pages 160–3)

... the interview
(see pages 166–91)

You don't get it
(see page 195)

The job is yours! It's time to
negotiate (see pages 193–5)

You start your new job
(see pages 198–208)

"The techniques that will help you get the right job are similar to those used by any business or organisation selling goods or services."

For others, the process will simply comprise sorting through curricula vitae (CVs), followed by an informal chat with the boss. Others will require potential recruits to complete a range of tasks. These may include one or several of the following:

- Application forms
- Covering letters
- Application supporting statements
- Psychometric tests
- Attending assessment centres
- Group tasks and away days
- Presentations or observations
- Panel interviews and one-on-one interviews.

Marketing yourself

Some employers require most of the application process to be completed online. Others prefer using referrals or networking to find new employees. Regardless of what recruitment techniques an employer chooses to use, he or she is always looking for the same thing: someone who appears to be the perfect person for the job. The techniques that will help you secure the right job are very similar to those used by any business or organisation selling goods or services. The only difference is that you will be selling yourself and your skills. To succeed, you will need to think about your market – your potential employers. Put yourself in their shoes. What do you think they are looking for? Can you match that profile, or if not, prove that with a bit of work, or a bit of time, you will be their perfect employee? The trick is to give yourself a fighting chance by presenting yourself in the best light. This means thinking about your appearance and your body language, as well as the look and content of any covering letter, CV or application form you submit.

If you have ever had an application turned down, it can feel demoralising. Try not to take it personally and don't let any setback affect your motivation. Analyse where you went wrong. Sort it out and apply for the next job. Remember that your recruiter desperately hopes that the next person to walk through the door will be the right person for the job.

Recruitment costs money. The process itself (advertisements, interviews, tests) and the potential losses incurred as long as the post remains empty will be a drain on the organisation looking for a new employee. They have a space that needs to be filled and you could be the one to fill it.

The job market

There is no point in applying for, and getting, any old job. If you are going to go to all the effort of job seeking, you may as well find something that is right for you. Don't waste time sending out applications all over the place in the hope that one will eventually work out for you. Use your time and energy in a focused and efficient way, only applying for work that you really want to do.

1

What do you want from a job?

Before you even start looking for work, it is important to think about what you want from a job. Do you have the skills and qualities needed to succeed in your application and, more vitally, to actually enjoy the job once you have got it?

We all work for very different reasons. For some of us, the most important thing is the money it pays. For others, a job is only good if it fits around school hours. Knowing what is right for you will help to narrow your search when you first enter the job market. So, when looking for a job, your first step should be to identify exactly what you want from it. Making a list and sticking to it at this stage will save you a lot of time and, possibly, heartache later on. If you really hate commuting, for example, but apply for a job that is well over an hour away from where you live, what will you do if you are offered the position? Will you compromise on the commuting and possibly regret your decision two months in? Or will you turn down the job offer? If so, perhaps it would have been a better use of your time and energy to focus on employment opportunities closer to home.

KEY AREAS

Key areas to consider when drawing up a list of criteria for your perfect job include:

- **Money.** Is there a minimum you need to earn in order to live comfortably? Is making as much money as possible important to you?
- **Commuting.** Does the distance from your home matter?
- **Prestige.** Does the name of your employer or your job title matter to you? Do you care whether your friends have heard of your organisation or not?
- **Ethics.** Are social, ethical or environmental issues important to you? Does your employer's approach need to echo your own values?
- **Involvement.** How involved do you want to be in the operation or politics of your job? Do you want to forget about it the moment you leave the office or would you prefer to be part of the strategic development team with a key say in the way your organisation grows?
- **Friendships.** Does your work need to provide you with opportunities for socialising? If you are new to a town

66 Criteria for your perfect job might include the pay, the location, the role and career prospects, and the employer's ethics. 99

and were hoping to make new friends at work, for example, would it be hard for you to be employed in a small business with perhaps just one or two colleagues?

- **Work/life balance.** Does your job need to fit around your home life? If looking after children or elderly relatives, could you cope with long hours or inflexible working practices?
- **Career development.** Do you want a job or a career? If you want to develop your career, would this position offer your training or promotion opportunities?

There may be other issues that are important to you, too. The key is to draw up your own list and apply it to any position that you might consider. If a job advertisement seems to fall short of your personal criteria, don't bother applying, there will be other opportunities and the last thing you want is to end up in a job in which you are unhappy or dissatisfied.

It may well be that money is not too much of a big issue for you. However, no matter how far down the list of criteria it appears, the bottom line is that you still need to earn enough to live on. To this end it is a good idea to research pay scales. Pay scales for roles in many professions such as teaching, accountancy and HR are accessible through their professional bodies. Recruitment agencies can also advise you on local salary bands. Employers often use a service called IDS Pay Benchmark, which provides information on going rates of pay for a wide range of jobs, but it is a fee-paying service. You could also check other local advertisements in your area for similar positions. However, it is worth remembering that many job advertisements give a 'package figure', which amounts to the salary plus benefits and some figures are dependent on whether you meet the sales targets.

Consider the bigger picture

In addition to listing what is important to you in a job, it is also worthwhile giving some thought to your career goals. If you want to build your career, you will need to decide on what you eventually want to achieve and then consider each employment opportunity as a stepping-stone on the way to your destination. Be strategic. When job-hunting, it may be wiser to consider sidesteps as well as looking for opportunities for promotion. A sidestep may help broaden your experience and widen your scope, ultimately providing you with more future opportunities.

 To find out more about the IDS Pay Benchmark service, which shows pay rates for many of Britain's leading employers, go to www.idspaybenchmark.co.uk.

YOUR PERSONAL SKILLS AND QUALITIES

When embarking on a job-hunt, you simply need to think about the job you would like to do and whether you fit the profile of someone suited to it. For example, there is little point in applying for a position as a gas engineer if you are not yet CORGI registered. By the same token, if you want to become a teacher, you will need a degree, either in education or in another subject together with a postgraduate certificate in education (PGCE). Before you start applying for anything, you should therefore find out exactly what qualifications you need.

A lack of qualification should not put you off entirely, however. It just means you will need to complete some training or education before you apply for the qualified position. You may also be able to find employment in a job that ultimately helps you reach your aim. For example, you could work as a plumber's mate while studying part-time for your CORGI certificate. Or you could work as a teaching assistant in a school while embarking on a teacher-training course or degree. In both of these examples, the experience that is gained while working part-time will help provide you with skills that will be useful to you when you finally secure the qualified position you are seeking. This is also something recognised by employers and will greatly enhance your CV.

In addition to thinking about what qualifications you may require, it is worthwhile taking some time to consider what a particular job actually entails and whether you possess the qualities needed to fulfil it. For example, you may have a good way with words and relish a career in a creative industry such as advertising. However, if the thought of public speaking fills you with horror, it is worth remembering that, in advertising, you would probably have to present your ideas or your work to colleagues and clients. This does not automatically mean that you would be no good in advertising. You may be fantastic. But be true to yourself. Would your shyness make you hate this job or is it something you feel you can deal with? You are the only person who can answer this question. And it is certainly something worth thinking about before you start applying for anything.

Making a list of your strengths and weaknesses, as well as your likes and dislikes, will also help you in your job search. But remember to write it down. Self-assessment is always hard as it is impossible to be truly objective, but by writing it down, you will help yourself focus on what you need to think about. Once you have narrowed down your options through a spot of self-analysis, you will be able to map out a career path or period of further training that will help you get where you want to be. One way to do this is to compare your list of qualities against job profiles. You may find such profiles listed in the careers offices of schools, colleges and universities, as well as on the website of the government-sponsored agency Learndirect (see box, opposite).

Case Study Sophie

Sophie left school with a handful of GCSEs. She also has a BTEC in business studies. She didn't enjoy studying business and wasn't sure what she wanted to do next. She knew that she needed to get a job, but she had no idea of what to do.

Before she even began looking for employment, however, she made a list of her strengths and weaknesses as well as her likes and dislikes. They read as follows:

Strengths
- I am calm and am good at calming other people when they are confused, flustered or frightened.
- I'm logical and good with numbers.
- I'm loyal and am prepared to work hard.

Weaknesses
- I'm not academic and I can find writing difficult.
- I have no work experience.
- I don't have many qualifications.

Likes
- I like dealing with people.
- I love all animals.

Dislikes
- I hate writing anything that someone else will read.
- I don't like the idea of working in an office or a shop.

Before writing this list, Sophie had only thought about the negatives.

- She felt that her lack of experience and few qualifications would limit her chances of getting something she would enjoy doing.
- She felt she was destined for shop work or to become an office junior like some of her friends.

The thought of this depressed her. However, after writing down her strengths and likes, she began to think of jobs that combined both. Nursing and customer services suited her people skills. If she wanted to include animals, she could work with a stable, an animal sanctuary, a zoo or a veterinary surgery.

Using the job profiles section of the learndirect website (see below), Sophie discovered a job she had never thought of before; a veterinary nurse (VN). Once she had decided what she wanted to do, she was able to start looking for a position with a Veterinary Nurse Approved Centre, which would allow her to complete work-based training. She knew it would involve study and exams, but she was so excited about the job that she resolved to study hard to become qualified.

Two years later, after completing her vocational training and passing some exams, Sophie qualified as a VN with the Royal College of Veterinary Surgeons.

 To access a large database of job profiles, see the advice section of the Learndirect website, www.learndirect-advice.co.uk.

PERSONALITY PROFILES

If you think analysing your own strengths and weaknesses could be useful to you, but don't know where to start, you could benefit from completing a personality questionnaire. The idea is that by identifying your major personality traits you can focus on the kinds of careers you would be best suited to. For example, if you enjoy working with information or like to deal with facts and ensure details are correct, you might excel in a career in accountancy or administration.

Don't let any supposed definition of your personality type put you off chasing your dream job, however. Just because you are not defined as being a 'thinker' this does not mean that you can't come up with great ideas. If you really want to do something, go for it. The chances are that your enthusiasm alone will help you to overcome any obstacles.

Some companies and organisations like to use personality profiles to help their staff understand how they work and

interact with colleagues, and may even use them to help resolve conflict. You will also find that many employers use a variety of **psychometric and ability tests** when recruiting.

Myers Briggs

There are several different types of test available that focus on personality, but one of the most popular is Myers Briggs. The concept was devised in the 1940s by Jungian psychologists Katharine Briggs and Isabel Briggs Myers. Their hypothesis is that people can be identified as belonging to one of 16 distinct personality types, made up of combinations of:

- Extraversion or introversion
- Sensing or intuition
- Thinking or feeling
- Judging or perceiving.

❝ Your personality traits might help you identify your ideal career, but if you really know what you want to do, go for it. ❞

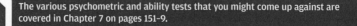

The various psychometric and ability tests that you might come up against are covered in Chapter 7 on pages 151–9.

All the types are regarded as equal, with no type being 'best'.

When applied to careers, the theory is that once you have defined what sort of personality you have, it will be easier for you to decide on what sort of jobs would best suit you. For example, if you have a preference for introversion, you may prefer a job that contains an element of research. If you prefer extraversion, you may enjoy a job that has plenty of interaction with people. Introversion and extroversion in these examples do not mean that you are an introvert or an extrovert exactly. 'Introversion' is a Myers Briggs label for someone who prefers to focus on his or her inner world as opposed to being more outward-looking.

The Psychological Testing Centre

The Psychological Testing Centre is part of the service provided by The British Psychological Society. It aims to set, promote and maintain standards in testing. To this end it currently offers training for, and Certificates of Competence in, various types of psychological testing, including those used by employers. If you come across a test that carries the Psychological Testing Centre logo, it will have been reviewed and registered by the Centre.

Other popular personality profilers include the Hogan Personality Inventory, Formula 4 Leadership and the Big Five Personality Test.

" The Myers Briggs test defines 16 personality types. None is the 'best'; all are regarded as equal, but you might identify your preferred role. "

Online sources of personality tests

- **www.myersbriggs.org** The Myers & Briggs Foundation, with information on the theory and options of where and how to take a Myers Briggs Test Instrument (MBTI) test.
- **http://resources.monster.com/tools** A variety of free online quizzes, including 'Discover your Perfect Career' from the online job board, Monster.
- **www.personalitytest.net** Information and access to online personality tests and quizzes.
- **www.outofservice.com** Fun and free personality quizzes online.
- **http://uk.tickle.com/career.html** Tests to help you evaluate your personality and your career options.

Climbing the career ladder

Unique challenges are presented at every point of the career ladder. If you are stepping onto the first rung, you will need to consider issues that are very different from someone who is reaching the highpoint of their career.

YOUR FIRST JOB

When you leave school, college or university and are just starting out, think big. So what if your careers adviser told you that media jobs were intensely competitive and hard to get? If that is what you want to do, go for it. If it is a competitive industry, you may enjoy the challenge as much as the career. Try not to be too hard on yourself, though. When mapping out your career path, remember that most people do not set out to do the job that they end up with. Life has a way of changing things. You may benefit from being in the right place at the right time and end up following a particular career path for lucky or pragmatic reasons. Or you may be unlucky. Changes in your personal circumstances may also change the way you think about your work.

Although looking for your first job may seem daunting and you can feel you are on the bottom of the heap, you are, in fact, in an incredibly strong position. Many organisations, both large and small, seek out school and college leavers or graduates to fill places on their training schemes or entry level positions. You hold the key to the future success of their business and competition for the best recruits is fierce.

Good grades will, of course, inevitably support any application you make, but the majority of employers also recognise that grades are not everything. They are looking for people who will make the transition from education to work as smoothly and quickly as possible. Employers are also looking for people who have passion and a drive to succeed. The key, therefore, is persuading employers that you have these qualities and that you will in some way enhance the value of their business or organisation.

 Putting together your first CV can seem especially daunting. See pages 86–91 where we provide you with tailor-made advice and some sample CVs.

Getting advice

Your first steps should include deciding on what you want to do. This is not just a question about what industry or sector you'd like to apply for jobs in today. If you are leaving school, ask yourself whether you really want to leave education. You will need to do this in the context of thinking about what career you would ultimately like to follow. It may be that you need a few more qualifications, perhaps A levels or NVQs, or even a degree. If you are not sure about what you want to do, speak to a careers adviser about your options. You should have one at your school or college. If not, one of your teachers should tell you how to contact one in your area.

Alternatively, you can find a careers adviser by contacting Connexions, if you live in England, or Careers Service Northern Ireland, Careers Wales and Careers Scotland if you live over the borders (see websites in the box below). Each of these agencies has offices located in towns and cities throughout the UK, staffed by careers advisers who should provide you with information so that you can make informed decisions. You can find the address of your local office in your telephone directory. A useful tool on each website enables you to research careers, so that you can browse jobs by occupation area. Each job summary should give you a good idea of what the work entails and what the pay is like, as well as information on training and the best entry routes.

If you are a university student or recent graduate, your first stop should be at your university's careers office. These offices are a fantastic source of advice, support and information, regardless of whether you do or don't know what to do. In addition, graduate websites such as www.prospects.ac.uk can help you map out a career path with online tools such as subject options, which list the possible career(s) available to people with your qualifications.

❝ Ask yourself what career path you want to follow in the long term. You may need to study for more qualifications. ❞

Online careers advice for students and young people

England www.connexions-direct.com
Wales www.careerswales.com
Scotland www.careers-scotland.org.uk
Northern Ireland www.careersserviceni.com
UK graduates www.prospects.ac.uk

Work experience

If you are a student, work experience or a work placement will do more for assisting you in your job-hunting attempts than any CV or application form. Try to complete a period of work experience before you start job-hunting, and before you leave school, college or university. If you have left already and are not succeeding in your hunt for a job, try to organise a period of work experience for yourself. In addition to looking great on your CV and being regarded as a definite plus point by recruiters, it will provide you with lots of useful information. This includes:

- Giving you a good flavour of a career or a business sector, which will help you decide whether you want a job in this area or not.
- Providing you with contacts for future references and recommendations.
- Enabling you to get a good idea of what an employer normally expects of an employee.

You may even impress your work experience employer so much that they offer you a job on completion of your studies. This can happen a lot as an employer can get a better idea of how well you are suited to a job when you are doing it than they can through reading your CV and interviewing you. This, of course, works both ways. If you are tempted by the thought of working for more than one employer and you can't decide which you prefer the look of, you could always try them out first with

a work placement. Nothing will give you a better flavour of what a particular employer is like to work for than actually doing so for a short period of time.

In recognition of the value of work experience, many universities and colleges have work placements as mandatory elements of some of their courses. If your course does not include this as part of the syllabus, consider using a gap year to provide you with paid or unpaid work experience. In addition to giving you valuable workplace and social skills, it will look better on a CV than a year spent lazing on a beach in Goa – although you could always spend half the year working and half the year travelling if that is what you want to do.

IF YOU ARE ALREADY EMPLOYED

The great thing about searching for a new job while you are currently employed is that you can operate from a position of confidence. While you are employed, you are earning money, so there is not the same urgency that someone who is unemployed faces. You do not need to rush the process just so that you have enough money to buy the basics or pay the bills. You can afford to look around and be fussy about what you apply for.

If your current job is well respected, it will reinforce the quality of your CV. Furthermore, if your current employer is desperate to keep you, you may find that any attempts you make to search for a new job are met with pay rises and perks. If this is the case, you will need to consider your reasons for looking for a new position carefully. Were you hoping to further your career by expanding your skills through the different demands of a new job? If you stay, will it have a negative effect on your career's growth? Or did you want to leave because you hate your job or your colleagues? Would a pay rise really make any difference if this is the case?

IF YOU ARE RETURNING TO WORK

There are probably nearly as many reasons for returning to work as there are returners. For the purposes of this book, the reasons are grouped into five common areas, each of which is discussed below, so that the issues and challenges that are distinctive to each can be examined. Remember that although these challenges may be unique to a particular group, they are probably not exclusive to you. Several websites have forums where you can discuss your concerns with other people in the same situation as you. The Learndirect website (www.learndirect.co.uk) has a forum where people, including returning mums, employees who left under a cloud and people who want to return to work after a period of sick leave, share their thoughts.

Agencies such as the not-for-profit organisation Tomorrow's People also focus on providing targeted help to the members of society throughout the UK who have the greatest difficulty in returning to work. Tomorrow's People (for details, see below) works with individuals with disabilities, ethnic minorities, lone parents, ex-offenders, the homeless and refugees.

Returning to work after caring for dependants

Many parents and carers report feeling a desperate lack of confidence at the thought of returning to work. If this describes you, try to remember that although you may not have been paid for what you did as a parent or a carer, you were still working and many of your skills are directly transferable to the workplace, as well as looking good on your CV. For example, if you have been looking after a child or an adult who is dependent on you, the chances are that you are organised, have good communication skills, are pretty good at dispute resolution and are brilliant at multi-tasking. It doesn't matter that being organised meant not forgetting the dates of doctors' appointments or school sports days. These are still skills that translate well into the workplace. You may find that you benefit from writing a CV that presents your skills and qualities in order of merit, rather than one that lists your life experience in chronological order.

 Tomorrow's People helps transform lives by getting individuals back into the workplace through targeted and specialist support. You can contact them through their website www.tomorrows-people.org.uk or by calling 01424 718491.

Examples of how to write different CVs are given in Chapter 4.

There are several sources of support and advice available for people who want to re-enter the job market after a period away from it. Your local Jobcentre Plus is a good place to start. Most towns and cities have their own Jobcentre Plus office. You can find the one nearest to you by looking in a telephone directory or by checking their website: see www.jobcentreplus.gov.uk. In addition to providing lists of job vacancies, they have specially trained advisers to provide you with advice and support. They will discuss your personal situation with you and together you can draw up a plan of action, which may involve a period of training or signing up to the New Deal for Lone Parents (see opposite), for example.

Childcare: There are several different types of childcare available to parents returning to work. Group care is provided by nurseries, crèches, out-of-school clubs and day-care centres. The majority of these are legally required to be registered with Ofsted (which completes regular on-site checks as well as police checks). One-to-one or small group care is provided by childminders, mother's helpers, nannies and au pairs. Only childminders currently need to be registered.

It is worth thinking about your needs and the needs of your child when trying to work out what would be the best for you. Childminders and nannies can often provide you with more flexible hours than a nursery and can keep siblings together regardless of their ages. A childminder or nanny can also look after your child in a home environment, rather than that of an institution. However, if your childminder or nanny goes on holiday, or is sick or looks after children of his or her own who are sick, you will need to find alternative childcare arrangements. Nurseries don't normally need to close due to staff sickness and often provide a wide range of equipment and activities, but they tend to be more expensive than childminders. Some children find it difficult to settle in the busy environment of a nursery.

You can claim back much of the costs of childcare through family credits, although this only applies to registered childcare providers. If you employ a nanny or you give some money to a relative who looks after your child, you will not be able to claim the costs back through tax credits or get tax relief on your childcare vouchers.

Once your child turns three, you are entitled to free nursery vouchers from the term after your child's third birthday. For many pre-school nurseries and playgroups, this will enable your child to

 For further information on tax credits, see the website of Her Majesty's Revenue & Customs (HMRC), www.hmrc.gov.uk, or call their helpline on 0845 300 3900.

Government initiatives to support working parents

The New Deal for Lone Parents

This is a government initiative rolled out through Jobcentre Plus. Through the scheme, single parents who wish to go back to work are assigned an adviser who helps with practical advice, such as how to find childcare and organise training. Your adviser also helps you apply for any work benefits and tax credit.

Child benefit

Child benefit is a tax-free regular payment made to anyone bringing up a child or young person. It isn't affected by your income or savings, so most people who bring up a child or young person can get it. You may be eligible if you are bringing up a child under the age of 16, or under 18 in full-time education or approved training.

Tax credits

These are available for most parents towards the cost of bringing up children and towards childcare costs for working parents. The child tax credit and working tax credit were introduced in April 2003 and replaced the working families' tax credit, disabled person's tax credit and children's tax credit.
- Child tax credit is a payment to support those families who are responsible for children, and 16- to 18-year-olds in full-time education (up to and including A levels, NVQ level 3 or equivalent). The amount you get is based on your household income. You can claim whether or not you are in work.
- Working tax credit supports working people (employed or self-employed and regardless of whether you have children or not) on low incomes by topping up earnings. It has several elements with the amount based on your circumstances. There are extra amounts for working at least 30 hours a week, working people who have a disability, and the costs of 'registered' or 'approved' childcare, known as the childcare element.

The Childcare Act

This was passed in 2006. It has given local authorities a set of duties that includes:
- Improving services for all pre-school children.
- Providing sufficient childcare provision for working parents.
- Ensuring that all parents have access to a local parental information service.

Registered childcare provision

For a list of registered childcare provision in your area (including childminders and nurseries), contact your local council. Telephone numbers for local councils or your local parental information service can be found in all telephone directories and most libraries. Alternatively, see www.childcarelink.gov.uk.

attend five sessions a week for free. A session lasts for two-and-a-half hours during a morning or an afternoon. However, the costs of some pre-school nurseries are higher than the vouchers allow for. If this is the case, or if you want your child to attend more than five sessions a week, you will need to make up the shortfall. Some schools also offer breakfast clubs and after school clubs offering a range of activities, although you normally have to pay for these.

Employment law rights: If you return to work while having dependants such as a child or an infirm relative, you also have several rights enshrined in employment law. These include time off for emergencies, where you are allowed to take reasonable amounts of unpaid leave to deal with situations such as when care arrangements break down or when an unexpected incident involving your child at school happens, for example.

Flexible working and the law

- **If you are a woman and are refused reduced hours of work (for example, on return to work after maternity leave), unless the employer can objectively justify the need to work on a full-time basis, this can be found to be unlawful indirect sex discrimination.**
- **Since April 2003, employers have had a legal duty to seriously consider requests for flexible working from parents of children under six, or 18 if disabled.**
- **Before making a complaint to the Employment Tribunal, you must usually make a formal grievance to your employer.**

If you have worked for the same employer for a year, you also have the right to unpaid parental leave. This allows you to take 13 weeks off work (in total, not per year) for each of your children up to their fifth birthday, or up to five years after the placement of an adopted child. You may also take up to 18 weeks for each disabled child you have, up to the child's eighteenth birthday. Furthermore, you have the right to request flexible working, although your employer may refuse this request. Attitudes to part-time work can be negative, so think about how you would phrase such a request to your employer. Working reduced hours may bring positive benefits to you and, by extension, to your workplace. Make sure you articulate this to your boss.

Working less than full-time: If you want to work less than full-time hours, there are three main ways you can do this: working part-time, job-sharing and voluntary reduced work time.

- *Working part-time* is the most common way that people in the UK balance work with other commitments. One in four people do it.
- *Job-sharing* is an arrangement where two people carry out the work that would normally be done by one person. Each person is employed on a part-time basis (either on a shared contract or an individual one) and divide up pay, holidays and benefits according to how much work they do. An estimated 4 per cent of the UK's workforce is employed in this way.

Further information for parents or carers who want to return to work

Changing Direction An organisation dedicated to helping people back to work after a career break. See www.changingdirection.com or call 020 8868 7818.

Mother at work Monthly webzine for working mothers; see www.motheratwork.co.uk.

Sure Start Government programme offering support to parents and children. See www.surestart.gov.uk or call their advice line 0870 000 2288.

Working Families A work-life balance organisation that campaigns for changes in the workplace and provides advice to working parents and carers. See www.workingfamilies.org.uk or call their advice line 0800 013 0313.

Other sources In addition to government organisations or companies charged with a remit by the government, such as learndirect, you can find support or advice in a variety of other sources and websites. Some of the websites have returning to work as their focus, such as:
- www. changingdirection.com or
- www.findmumajob. co.uk.

Others contain forums where people in a similar situation to you may share thoughts or ideas. If you have been caring for a child with cerebral palsy, for example, you may benefit from a discussion on returning to work with other carers on the Scope website: www.scope.org.uk.

- *Voluntary reduced working time* allows people to reduce working hours for a specific period, say a year, after which the employee has the right to return to full-time employment. You may find this works for you if you want to work a four-day week on return from maternity leave, for example. Or perhaps you might find work easier if you could have your daily hours reduced from eight to seven so that you can enjoy a bit of extra time in the evenings to care for an elderly relative.

Unpaid leave: If you are employed and are pregnant or are planning to adopt a child, you are entitled to 52 weeks paid and unpaid maternity or adoption leave. The amount you receive depends on how much you earned and how long you worked for prior to your leave and how long you plan to take off. For further details see www.direct.gov.uk.

❝ You may want to reduce your working hours for a year and then return to full-time employment, or perhaps you'd find work easier if you could reduce your daily hours from eight to seven. ❞

Work after retirement

According to figures published at the end of 2006 by Labour Force Statistics, more than one million people work beyond state pension age, representing 11 per cent of people over the age of 65 years. Although less than the USA, the UK has one of the highest proportions of older people in work in the European Union, only coming after Sweden and Denmark.

Despite these positive statistics, however, many older people find returning to work difficult. In addition to advances in technology and working practices, some people experience difficulties with age discrimination. According to a survey by Kelly Global Workforce Index, more than 50 per cent of people over the age of 45 felt that they had been discriminated against because of their age.

Updating your skills: One of the greatest hurdles faced by older people trying to go back to work after retirement is ensuring their skills are up to date and ready for our contemporary workplace. This is not insurmountable and there are plenty of agencies prepared to help you. The government's New Deal suite of support includes a scheme aimed at the over-50s. If you are in this age bracket and have been claiming one of several benefits, such as pension credit, you can receive a dedicated programme to help you get a job. The scheme is accessible through your local Jobcentre Plus office. Charitable organisations such as Age Concern and The Age and Employment Network (TAEN, formerly known as the Third Age Employment Network), also provide support and advice for people looking for work after retirement (see box, opposite, for more information).

Regardless of the challenges you face, always bear in mind how much value your experience brings to the workplace. No amount of training or qualifications can provide that, and it is one area where you have the edge over a younger applicant.

❝ Many older people find returning to work difficult because of changes to technology, working practices, or age discrimination. ❞

 If you feel that you have been discriminated against because of your age, seek legal advice. Find your local Citizens Advice Bureau via the website www.adviceguide. org.uk or contact the Age Concern freephone Information Line on 0800 00 99 66.

Further information for older people who want to return to work

Age Positive Campaign working within the Department of Work and Pensions, supporting older people into employment, see www.agepositive.gov.uk or call 0113 232 4444.
Age Concern Charity supporting the needs of older people, with advice on returning to work after retirement, see www.ageconcern.co.uk or call their information line 0800 00 99 66.
The Age and Employment Network A charity that supports job-seekers in their mid and later life, see www.taen.org.uk or call 020 7843 1590.

Returning to work after redundancy or dismissal

Looking for a new job after having been made redundant or dismissed from a company or organisation can seem like a depressing prospect. Perhaps you feel betrayed by the firm that let you go, or maybe you feel that you possessed more qualities than someone who was retained. And who on earth would want to employ you again if you have been sacked?

There is no point in brooding on these issues. Why not try to put the past behind you and concentrate on improving your future? And if that means earning a living, try to find a job that you will enjoy.

If you have been dismissed, you will need to think carefully about how you explain yourself on your CV. Whatever you do, don't lie. Providing false information could result in your dismissal for gross misconduct (and two dismissals in a row could make your CV even trickier to write). However, you do need to give yourself a fighting chance:

- Avoid giving reasons for leaving your previous position on your CV, allowing you to explain yourself more fully in person during the interview.

- If you have to complete an application that requests a reason for leaving previous employment, you could try to get around it by saying there are several reasons that merit fuller explanation.

In truth, unless the rest of your CV is outstanding, it is unlikely that you would be invited to interview if you list one or more dismissals for gross misconduct without adequate explanation. If you were dismissed during a probationary period, be honest and admit that it was not the right job for you and, if possible, explain that was a decision that you came to in mutual agreement with your boss.

If you were sacked for gross misconduct, your prospective new employer will want to be reassured that it was a one-off and will not happen again. One good tip is to apply through a third party, such as an employment agency, who could argue your case in a dispassionate and balanced way.

Redundancy outplacement: If you are made redundant, it is likely that your company will go to great lengths to help you find new work. This is to help

Further information following redundancy or dismissal

Fired from your job Advice on UK employment law, see www.iambeingfired.co.uk.
Resigning from your job Information and advice on how to find work after leaving your job, see www.i-resign.com/uk.

Jobcentre Plus Support and advice for job seekers; to find out more about the organisation and the location of your local office, look them up in your local telephone directory or see www.jobcentreplus.gov.uk.

minimise the blow to you and any negative effects on the morale of the workforce that remains. Your organisation is only legally obliged to look for alternatives for you within the company. However, many employers refuse to abandon you entirely and often ask specialists to help you. These may be outsourced, or they may be from your own HR department.

The type of help you receive can vary, but typically you would be invited to attend an outplacement workshop designed to help you through the recruitment process. You may be given tips on where to find work, help on writing or updating your CV and advice on how to handle interviews and assessment centres.

Starting work after a period of ill health or disability

If you want to return to work but are still not quite strong enough to carry on where you left off, consider going back on a part-time basis to begin with. An occupational therapist could advise you and your employer on any physical changes to your work station to make things easier for you. Or you may benefit from entering work through a 'social firm' or an employment scheme that offers sheltered or supported employment. Many of these schemes are run by charities (such as Rethink, the Shaw Trust, the Stort Trust and United Response), and the government (Remploy) (see box on page 30 for more information).

Some hospitals and clinics run rehabilitation services, which provide advice and support on how to get back into work. Some charities and not-for-profit organisations provide employment advice tailored to illnesses or disabilities in their own specific areas, such as the mental health organisation, Mind, or the RNID, which works with people who have hearing impairment or deafness. Both Mind and the RNID contain good information and advice on their websites (see also box on page 30).

 If you do feel low, do what you can to pep yourself up and read up on body language and attitude in Chapter 7.

The government's New Deal for Disabled People focuses on trying to make returning to work easier for people who have experienced health problems or disability. This scheme is run by your local Jobcentre Plus.

Benefits: Your job centre should also provide you with information on benefits. You may be worried that if you start back in employment and, for whatever reason, it does not work out that you forfeit your benefits. However, it is possible for many people to continue to receive benefits as they start back at work. Many job centres have an in-house Disability Employment Adviser (DEA), who should be able to advise you on all aspects of finding and keeping a job, as well as working out your benefits with you and helping you to access different schemes as appropriate. Alternatively, contact your local Citizens Advice Bureau or benefits office.

The Disability Discrimination Act (DDA): This was passed in 1995 and then significantly updated in 2005. It is designed to protect disabled people from discrimination in employment, as well as other areas. Under the terms of the Act, employers are legally required to make any reasonable adjustments to their place of work to accommodate anyone who has a disability (see box, below). Any employer that displays the Disability Symbol (right) has agreed to meet certain commitments to employ, retain and develop the careers of people with disabilities. These include the promise to interview all applicants with a disability who meet the minimum criteria for a particular job, and that they will consider them on their individual merit for the job in question.

Reasonable adjustments to accommodate anyone with a disability

These may include:
- Changes to your workplace to improve access or layout.
- Giving some of your duties to another person, for example employing a temp or reallocating some tasks.
- Changing your working hours, for example allowing flexi-time, a job-share, starting later or finishing earlier.
- Time off for treatment, assessment or rehabilitation.
- Additional training for you and for your colleagues (who may need to learn how to accommodate your needs).
- Getting new or adapting existing equipment (such as chairs, desks, computers, vehicles).
- Modifying instructions or procedures, for example by providing written material in bigger text or in Braille.
- Improving communication, for example providing a reader or interpreter, having visual as well as audible alarms.

Health issues: If you are not asked specifically about your health during the recruitment process, you are not legally obliged to disclose any serious health issues in your past. However, if you are questioned on your health, or about a gap in your employment history, do be honest as it is important that your work does not have a bad effect on your health. Employers should be willing to make reasonable adjustments to the workplace to help people with disabilities get into work or stay in work. For further advice on disclosure, contact your local Citizens Advice Bureau. Some charities also provide excellent advice in this area.

Looking for work after release from prison

According to the Prison Reform Trust, every year 90,000 prisoners are released from jail in England and Wales but of this number, only about 25 per cent have a paid job lined up to go to. If you are one of the 75 per cent majority facing unemployment, the task of finding a job may seem impossible. But don't despair. If employers consider your conviction to be irrelevant to the job, many of them have no problem in employing ex-offenders. Alternatively, you could find a job with someone who knows you or who has received a verbal recommendation about you, who may be

---

Further information for job seekers with ill health or a disability

Commission for Equality and Human Rights New agency that has replaced the Disability Rights Commission (also taking on the work of the former Equal Opportunities Commission and Commission for Racial Equality). It provides advice and information for disabled people; see www.equalityhumanrights.com.

Employment Opportunities for People with Disabilities A charity dedicated to creating routes into employment for people with disabilities and medical conditions; see www.opportunities.org.uk.

Mind The National Association for Mental Health in the UK, campaigns on behalf of those with mental illness; see www.mind.org.uk.

Remploy A specialist employment service that finds employment opportunities for people with disabilities; see www.remploy.co.uk.

Rethink Providers of a range of practical support and information, including advice on employment and training, for people with mental health problems; see www.rethink.org.

RNID Campaigning charity for people with hearing impairment, provides services, training, information and support; see www.rnid.org.uk.

Shaw Trust Largest voluntary sector provider of employment services for disabled people in the UK; see www.shaw-trust.org.uk.

Social Firms UK Creates employment opportunities for disadvantaged people; see www.socialfirms.co.uk.

United Response Support for people with learning difficulties and mental health problems including access to training and work opportunities; see www.unitedresponse.org.uk.

more confident about your skills and reliability than they would about an unknown applicant with no criminal record. Any jobs you apply for after this will be much easier, as you should be able to show a good working record and provide a good reference.

There are also several agencies whose very existence revolves around providing you with practical advice, support and mentoring. Some organisations even work within prisons, helping offenders prepare for employment in advance of their release date.

Disclosure of your record: Legally, you do not have to disclose your criminal

record unless you are asked about it. And in most cases you do not have to disclose it at all if it becomes 'spent' (where it can be forgotten after a certain period of time). The length of your sentence dictates how much time must pass before your conviction becomes spent, but on average it is about seven years. The Rehabilitation of Offenders Act 1974 does contain some exceptions. This includes any job that involves working with children or vulnerable adults and certain professions, such as law, health, security and financial services. For guidance and a full list of exempt careers, contact the probation service or an organisation such as NACRO (see box, below).

Further information for job seekers with a criminal record

National Association for the Care and Resettlement of Offenders (NACRO) Provides information and support on many issues including employment, training and education; see www.nacro.org.uk or call their resettlement helpline for ex-offenders: 0800 0181 259.

Offender Learning and Skills Service (OLASS) A service offered by the Learning and Skills Council, provides you with access to training; see http://olass.lsc.gov.uk/.

Prison Advice and Care Trust (PACT) Provides resettlement services, contact advice desk in court or advisers in prison; see www.prisonadvice.org.uk or call 020 7490 3139.

Resettlement, Education, Support, Employment and Training (RESET) Resettlement support for young offenders. Speak to someone in your local youth offending team; see www.reset.uk.net or call 020 7840 5615.

Tomorrow's People Helps disadvantaged people from many areas, including ex-offenders, find work. Find the centre closest to you in your local telephone directory; see www.tomorrowspeople. org.uk, or call 01424 718 491.

Women in Prison (WIP) Resettlement support for women offenders; see www.womeninprison.org.uk or call 020 7226 5879.

Criminal records checks, sometimes called CRB (criminal records bureau) checks, or standard disclosures, enhanced disclosures and basic disclosures were introduced in 2002. If your prospective employer asks for one of these checks as a condition of your recruitment, your conviction and possibly (depending on the level of the check) information, such as cautions or final warnings, will be revealed to them.

❝ Legally, you do not have to disclose your criminal record unless you are asked about it. ❞

What next?

To get started on your journey towards new employment, work through each of the points below.

1 Consider what you want from a job and any long-term career goals you may have.

2 Write down all of your qualifications, skills and qualities.

3 Record your strengths and weaknesses, likes and dislikes. Compare them and your goals and qualifications to job profiles in your chosen industry. From this, draw up a shortlist of positions that may suit you.

4 Think about any special needs your personal circumstances require. Are you a recent graduate? Or are you looking for work after a career break? Investigate what targeted support and advice may be available to you from a variety of agencies.

Once you have worked through these steps, you will have narrowed down exactly what you would like to do and you will have a summary of your greatest selling features. Read on to find some of the best sources you can use to find work.

First steps

Job opportunities can appear from anywhere and job vacancies may be advertised in a variety of places, from agencies and careers offices to the press and online. If you are going to succeed in getting a job, you will need a good idea of where to look for one. And if you can't find an advertisement for what you want, you can always bypass the whole search procedure, go straight to the employer directly and ask them to employ you.

2

Where to find job vacancies

Before you can even begin to write your CV, fill in an application form or prepare for an interview, you need to find a job vacancy you can apply for. There are a wide range of sources where you might find work advertised. You will increase your chances if you look at as many as possible.

THE PRESS

The two most common places to find jobs advertised are in newspapers and on the internet (see below). Newspapers are the traditional source of many job advertisements and used to be the most popular place for employers to advertise. In a 2007 survey carried out by the Chartered Institute of Personnel and Development (CIPD), it was revealed that corporate websites had broken even with local newspaper advertisements as the most common method of attracting candidates.

National newspapers

Virtually all of the nationals publish lists of job vacancies, many of which are included in subject-specific supplements. For example, *The Guardian* publishes job advertisements for creative, media, sales, marketing, public relations, secretarial and administration jobs every Monday in a supplement called *MediaGuardian*. All the newspapers that run classified recruitment advertising also publish **job boards** online. To access them, go to the website of each paper and follow the relevant links.

In addition, *The Times* and *The Guardian* also publish supplements devoted to the subject of how to manage your career. *The Times Career* appears every Thursday. It also has a useful website (www.timesonline.co.uk/career), which carries information from both the weekday and *The Sunday Times* including the Top 100 Graduate Employers, the Top 50 Places to Work for Women and tips on how to succeed in particular sectors such as banking or

Jargon buster

Job board An online listing of job vacancies, often published by newspapers or by dedicated websites such as Monster

 Further information about online recruitment, including job boards (both those of newspapers and large independent job boards such as Monster), can be found in Chapter 3 and contact details are given on page 214.

regeneration'. *The Guardian* publishes two supplements called *Work* and *Graduate* that appear on Saturdays. These contain articles on a wide range of work-related subjects, such as how to succeed in a job-share, or answering the question: 'Will a Master's degree help me find a career in sports marketing?' *The Guardian* publishes these sections online at www.guardian.co.uk/money/work and www.guardian.co.uk/money/graduates.

Local newspapers

Local newspapers are also a good source of job advertisements. Local dailies often only publish classified job advertisements one day a week, however, so it is worth checking which day this is before you head off to buy a paper. Some local papers are weekly and many are free.

Trade press

If you are thinking about furthering your career, you might already subscribe to some of the magazines that specialise in your area. If not, it is well worth having a look at one or two. Most large newsagents and libraries will carry some and many will be available through your sector's unions. The advantage of searching for job vacancies in a trade or speciality magazine is that the majority of advertisements will be in areas you are interested in, or have experience and expertise in. Some of the larger

magazines and trade newspapers, such as *The Nursing Times* or the *Times Educational Supplement (TES)* also have websites where sector jobs are advertised.

Classified press

Publications devoted to classified advertising, such as *Loot,* carry many job advertisements. In addition to publishing several local variations (including *Loot London*, *Loot Manchester* and *Loot Liverpool*), the *Loot* stable also includes *London Recruit* and *Jobs Week*. The latter is published in association with www.jobsite.co.uk and London's *Evening Standard* and *Metro* newspapers.

CAREERS FAIRS

A careers fair or **milkround** is an event where prospective employers are brought together under one roof to advertise their company and meet possible recruits. They represent an excellent opportunity for you to meet potential employers face-to-face. Even if you haven't completed your studies, a careers fair

Jargon buster

Milkround A careers fair held at a university or college of higher education. The name was coined because just like a milkman delivers milk to your door, a graduate recruiter delivers jobs to your university

 To see online jobs for *The Nursing Times* and the TES, go to www.nursingtimes.net and www.tes.co.uk.

is a valuable source of information, contacts and interview experience.

Careers fairs, exhibitions and milkrounds tend to be aimed at undergraduates and graduates, but not exclusively so. The *British Medical Journal* (BMJ), for example, regularly organises careers fairs that are aimed at medical professionals regardless of their grade, speciality or location. In common with many careers exhibitions, the BMJ careers fairs are not just a chance for employers to showcase vacant situations, they also host seminars on such subjects as interview skills, CV writing, application forms, working abroad and working outside of the NHS. Individual exhibition stands also provide careers advice, information on how to find a new job and how to identify alternative career pathways.

Jobcentre Plus also organises job fairs. Just like any other careers fair, these fairs are designed to give job seekers the chance to meet and talk to employers. Anyone can attend a Jobcentre Plus jobs fair, you do not have to be registered unemployed to visit one. To find out about the next job fairs to be held in your area, contact your local Jobcentre Plus office.

Most undergraduate and graduate recruitment fairs are held at universities and colleges. Some fairs group together clusters of universities and colleges, such as the London Graduate Recruitment Fair or the Liverpool Graduate Careers Fair. Others focus on a sector or skills specialism, such as the Management, Finance and Business Fair in Leicester. Some fairs have a national focus, including the National Graduate Recruitment Exhibition held at the NEC in Birmingham.

What a careers fair can do for you

Just like the seminars and events held at the BMJ National Fair, many university careers fairs present a useful and often practical range of careers advice, seminars and presentations. In addition, a fair provides you with the opportunity to expand your network, both with recruiters and other graduates. It enables you to learn more about an industry or sector, as well as giving you the chance to gather information about individual companies. Even if you are not interested in the exhibitors, a careers fair could provide you with access to useful careers information and allow you to hone your interview skills by talking to employers. At the very least this should help you with your confidence and prepare you for the time when you talk to an employer you do want to work for.

Finding a careers fair

To find out details of upcoming careers fairs, you can contact the careers advice offices of individual universities and

Websites for the careers fairs mentioned are: www.bmj.com, www.londongradfair. co.uk, www.liverpoolfairs.org.uk, www.le.ac.uk and www.necgroup.co.uk.

colleges, or see websites such as www.prospects.ac.uk or www.milkround.com, which have fairly comprehensive listings. If you would like to meet a particular company at a careers fair, give them a call and ask which fairs they will be attending. They may even schedule a meeting with you.

Some employers recruit directly from careers fairs, so it pays to take the events seriously and arrive at them well prepared (see below).

> **❝ Many careers offices offer coaching in employability skills plus support and advice for several years after you graduate. ❞**

CAREERS OFFICES

Most schools, colleges and universities have a careers office or a career development unit. At the very least, these offices should be able to give you careers advice designed to help you choose which courses to study in order to equip you with the skills or qualifications you need for a particular career. Many do much more than this, offering coaching in employability skills, information including employers' brochures on graduate recruitment schemes, and organising employer presentations and workshops. Many continue to offer support and advice for several years after you have graduated. You can normally access face-to-face advice from an experienced careers adviser, as well as benefit from telephone and email services.

Some universities that offer MBA degrees also provide a careers service especially for MBA students. This typically could include the opportunity to

How to prepare for a careers fair

- Find out in advance which firms will be there and research the ones you are interested in talking to. You will come across much better if you appear to know a bit about the firm.
- Dress smartly, as you would for an interview.
- Bring plenty of copies of your CV, both to give out to prospective employers and to benefit from any CV workshops that the event may run.
- If appropriate, bring examples of your work. A graphic design agency, for instance, may like to see your portfolio of artwork.
- Don't overlook the smaller fairs. Some big employers still attend and you might get more chance to talk at a less busy fair.
- Visit your favourite company third or fourth. This gives you a chance to warm up and practise on a few other firms first.

undertake psychometric tests, one-to-one coaching workshops, networking events and work placements.

Student Unions

Your university's careers office is not the only place where you can find jobs on campus. Many student unions have job boards (literal as opposed to online ones), where local employers looking for part-time workers advertise for jobs. This is a particularly good place to find work if you are looking for a part-time or casual job to supplement your student loan.

JOBCENTRE PLUS

Jobcentre Plus is a government agency that helps anyone out of work to find a job. Touch-screen 'Jobpoints' in every office give you access to the country's biggest job bank, advertising job vacancies both around the UK and overseas.

In addition to job advertisements placed directly by employers, Jobcentre Plus offices advise people on what social benefits (such as working tax credit) they may be eligible for. You may also be eligible for one of the New Deal initiatives. This is a government programme that specialises in providing targeted back-to-work help and support to certain groups of people. These include:

- Young people
- Single parents
- Musicians
- Long-term unemployed people over the age of 25 years
- People with disabilities
- The partners of people in receipt of benefits
- People who are aged over 50 years.

Jobcentre Plus job-hunters are normally assigned an adviser to provide help and advice tailored to your situation. They discuss potential vacancies to narrow down a list of possible jobs or areas that you may be suited to. They may also provide practical help on how to write a CV and a covering letter. They explore skills training opportunities with you or help you with practical problems, such as how to find suitable childcare. The Jobcentre Plus website (see below) contains a range of information and advice, including interview preparation and writing letters. It also has a large database of job vacancies, both in the UK and in Europe.

Jobseeker Direct

Your local Jobcentre Plus office may also put you in touch with another government-sponsored service, Jobseeker Direct. This is a telephone service charged at local rates (see below). Your adviser will help you find the right job for you, tell you how to apply, send you an application form and, where possible, ring the employer to arrange an interview.

 The Jobcentre Plus website is www.jobcentreplus.gov.uk. To contact Jobseeker Direct, telephone 0845 606 0234 or textphone 0845 605 525 if you have a hearing or speech impairment.

Reading a job advertisement

Once you have found a vacancy for a job you want, it's time to get down to details. How do you read the advertisement and how do you match your skills to it?

INTERPRETING AN ADVERTISEMENT

So what do job advertisements really mean? If an advertisement requires you to be 'flexible', does it mean you have to be prepared to work long hours? If it is looking for a motivated self-starter, does this mean that you just have to get on with things and will receive no training, no support and no feedback? Possibly it will mean this, though not necessarily. If an advertisement demands flexibility, it might just mean that your employer would like you to cover for the receptionist while she or he is on lunch. The need for a self-motivator might just mean that they don't want to have to give you a task list every morning.

If you find yourself asking what an advertisement means, it isn't doing its job properly. It might not be trying to con you into thinking that a job is better than it really is, it might just be poorly written. Either way, if you come across a vague

advertisement, it is worth thinking about it very carefully before you apply. Ask yourself these questions. Is it:

- Vague because the employer does not know what they want you to do?
- Difficult to understand because the employer is trying to mask the fact that the job isn't great?
- Unclear because the employer is slapdash and does not care about quality or image?

One easy way to clear up any confusion is to call and ask. If your prospective employers are unable to tell you on the phone what they mean when they say they are looking for someone who is 'flexible', steer well clear. Not only might you waste your time going to the effort of completing an application for a job that you are not suited for, but also if you get the job, you could end up working for an awful employer. As an employee, you deserve more.

Selling the post

That said it is worth remembering that a job advertisement is just that, advertising. It is specifically designed to make you want to buy in to what they are selling,

❝ Beware of responding to unclear advertisements, as the employer may not know what they want. ❞

39

in this case a job. Many companies don't even write the advertisements themselves, they pay copywriters or advertising agencies to do it for them. The brief is always to make the company sound as good as possible. It is not just job-hunters that see job advertisements. Shareholders, customers and competitors see them too, which makes them as important as an advertisement that sells the company's product or service.

And what is more, the role of a job advertisement is a bit more sophisticated than a regular advertisement, which wants as many customers as possible to buy a product. An employer looking for a new recruit does not want to sift through thousands of applications for one job, especially if most of them are ill-suited or unqualified for the position. The role of the job advertisement, therefore, is to attract a manageable number of the most suitable candidates.

But how does this help you? The key is to be a savvy reader and look through each advertisement carefully. Look for advertisements that seem to talk to you and your specific set of skills and qualities. Think about the company placing the advertisement. Have you heard of it? Does it have a good reputation or good prospects? If the job sounds promising but the company is unknown to you, search it out on the internet or check out newspaper archives

in your local library (the librarians can help direct your research if you tell them what you are looking for).

- **Be wise to the falseness of many job titles.** Despite the grandness of the title 'executive', it can often be used to refer to employees on the bottom of the scale. An account executive, for example, is often someone whose position is below both that of account manager and account director. If you already are an account manager in your current firm, do you really want to apply for a position below the one you are in?
- **Beware any advertisements** you see from the same company appearing with great frequency. It probably means the company has a high staff turnover.
- **Consider the entire package.** A job vacancy may not offer quite what you were hoping to be paid, but if a car, company pension and health insurance are part of the package, think carefully about what those perks are worth to you.
- **Bear in mind that a job advertisement** is subject to the same legal controls as other advertisements. Employers are not allowed to make false claims about what they are offering, and if they do, it might be worth seeking legal advice with the Citizens Advice Bureau.

 The website for the Citizens Advice Bureau is www.adviceguide.org.uk, which is their online service providing independent advice on your rights.

Use the advertisement to help your application

Don't be despondent if a job advertisement asks for so many qualities that only a fictional superhero could fit the bill. A company is hardly going to advertise for someone who is lazy, grumpy and lacking in all qualifications. Imagine it as a game of pairs. The company has laid out its hand of cards; all you have to do is match your hand to theirs.

- **Note the qualities and/or skills** that the advertisement demands as 'essential', which are normally used as a quick screening process. A haulage company seeking lorry drivers may include a requirement for people with a full HGV licence. This works as a good pre-selector, screening out inappropriate applicants before they even apply. If someone without the necessary licence applies anyway, he or she will end up in the rejection pile straight away. If you don't meet any of the 'must have' requirements in an advertisement, don't bother applying, it will be a waste of your time. However, saying that, it also depends on what the employer wants you to have the skills for. An HGV licence is cut and dried. If you don't have one, you legally won't be able to drive their lorries.

- **Question the wording.** For example, what if the employer states that at least two years' experience is essential? Always ask yourself, 'What do they want that for?' In the case of two years' experience, it is likely that the employer does not want new starters or recent graduates. If it is for a job where a skilled operator is required, the issue is being able to use the equipment properly, not the number of years.

- **Use this kind of information** to support your application, demonstrating how you personally fit the skills requirement, even if not in the way demanded by the advertisement. For example, if you are a qualified lorry driver with just one year of experience, you could point out in your application that during that year you gained experience in several different areas, including on the road, in building sites and a quarry. If you are also able to demonstrate the level of your skills, perhaps in this case with a safe driver award from a previous employer, the need for two years would probably be overlooked.

- **Back up your application with examples.** When an advertisement asks for a candidate that is 'flexible', list examples of situations in which you have been flexible; perhaps you ran the account of a colleague as well as your own accounts, when he or she was away sick. If it demands strong analytical skills and interpersonal skills, demonstrate yours with a real-life example. Analytical skills may include experience in book-keeping; interpersonal ones may include entertaining clients. You may also consider illustrating your skills with examples from outside of the working

41

environment. Your interpersonal skills, for example, may be best illustrated with your membership of various sports teams.

In short, when you look at the requirements that are listed in a job advertisement, don't just consider them as a tick list of your qualifications and qualities. Use them as a prompt to help you write a targeted CV and letter in which you demonstrate all or most of the qualities your prospective employer is looking for.

❝Use the listed requirements as a prompt to help you write a targeted CV and letter designed to meet the employer's needs.❞

Types of job

- **Full-time** This is generally classified as a job where you work a minimum of 31 hours a week.
- **Part-time** This is generally classified as a job where you work less than 30 hours a week.
- **Permanent** A full-time or part-time job that does not have a fixed end date. You have the right to continue working there until you choose to move on, or you are made redundant or sacked, or your retire.
- **Fixed-term contract** A full-time or part-time job that lasts for a pre-agreed period. This may be in terms of time, for example six months, or until the completion of a project, for example the implementation of a new computer system. Fixed-term

contracts are often used to employ temporary cover for an employee on maternity leave.
- **Temporary** This applies to any job that is not permanent. It could be a fixed-term contract or it may be work that you complete per shift, perhaps covering for a permanent member of staff who is off sick or on holiday.
- **Freelance** Freelance workers are self-employed and sell their services to a variety of employers. They are governed by different laws on tax and employment (for example they do not have sick pay or holiday entitlements paid to them by their clients and they are not taxed under a PAYE system).

Alternative routes to jobs

A large proportion of job vacancies are not advertised. To truly succeed in the job market, you will need to know when this is the case, and how to get around it.

Occasions where a job is not advertised may include positions where:

- An employer doesn't want to pay for a costly recruitment campaign.
- An employer trusts someone they know more than they would an anonymous applicant.
- It might be commercially sensitive for a company to reveal it is recruiting.
- Fierce competition in a popular industry allows employers to cherry pick from a ready pool of recommendations.

Many employers choose not to advertise their employment vacancies because they prefer a recruitment agency or a headhunter to find suitable candidates for them. This is such a big area of recruitment we have devoted all of Chapter 6 to the subject.

NETWORKING

How do you find a job that is not advertised, or is not advertised in the places you are looking? Apart from cold calling prospective employers, which we examine in more detail later, you could use your own network of friends, family, colleagues, clients and acquaintances. Networking helps. In fact, when it comes to recruitment, it is one of the most popular ways of finding employees. Employers like to use networks because it helps them find a known quantity. If you are known and trusted by a contact of the employer, you are likely to be more attractive than someone who is not known to them personally. This can be really useful if your CV has employment gaps or is not as strong as it could be.

A network can operate in two directions. The people within it can spread the word among their own acquaintances that you are hunting for work or work experience. They can also let you know about any employers who may be looking for new employees. You can even use your network to find out what is happening within your chosen marketplace.

- Are there any trends that may affect employment?
- Has one major firm merged with another?
- Has this resulted in redundancies or new recruitment?

Having a broader understanding of your industry and the major players within it will help you appear knowledgeable in your interview. It will also help you in your general career development if you have a good idea of who is who, and what is happening where. Discussing such issues among a range of contacts in your industry will help foster both your general and your inside knowledge.

How to network

When networking, you are not asking directly for a job, but are scouting around finding out what may be available and any trends that may be developing. This is easier than asking for a job directly and yet it can still yield positive results. Don't just stop at the people you know, speak to the people they know too. Ask for introductions. For example, you may ask your uncle who works in the catering industry if he could put you in touch with anyone who employs pastry chefs.

When you call your uncle's contact, explain that he suggested you call and that you wanted to ask about the

recruitment policies of your contact's company. If your contact is willing, you could develop this into a more general conversation about career opportunities for chefs in your area. It is possible that a more general conversation may reveal opportunities elsewhere. For example, if you ask whether the Grand Hotel is recruiting, the answer is likely to be no. However, if you talk about opportunities for pastry chefs in Bournemouth, you may find out that there are no vacancies at the Grand, but that the Metropolitan is due to open a new restaurant within the next few months and may start recruiting new kitchen staff soon.

Approach networking in a systematic and organised manner. The easiest way to do this is to make a list. Write down a list of people you know and feel comfortable about approaching. They do not need to work in the industry you work in. After all, the whole idea is that they know someone who does. So, make two lists:

- One that includes family, friends, colleagues, associates and, if this is possible, clients.
- A second one that outlines who you have talked to and whether they have given you any leads.

If a colleague has suggested you speak to a friend of theirs, you will need to

Networking online

Online forums are an ideal place to practise such networking techniques and a whole new industry has grown up around the idea. Social networking sites such as Facebook (www.facebook.com) and Bebo (www.bebo.com) are increasingly popular and Facebook, in particular, is frequently used by professionals seeking job openings and new employment opportunities.

For more information about online social networking, see Chapter 3.

remember who put you in touch with whom. So keep careful notes. As your network grows, the links between people can become increasingly complicated. Your colleague's friend, John Smith, may be unknown to you. If he then puts you in touch with another unknown, Anne Jones, you will need to remember who she is and the link that brought you to her. If you have kept careful notes, when you first contact Anne Jones you can say, 'John Smith suggested I call you.'

TEMPORARY POSITIONS

Work placements, voluntary work, temporary contracts and working in a role related to the one you want are all excellent ways of getting closer to your career goals. These methods are particularly useful in careers such as the media, or even the not-for-profit sector where competition for jobs is fierce.

Many employers do not advertise temporary jobs in newspapers or job boards, but use recruitment agencies to find staff for them. If you are keen on working in an industry where very few vacancies are advertised, look for a recruitment agency that specialises in your field. Remember to offer yourself as available for full-time or part-time work, temporary or permanent positions.

Temporary contracts

If you want to work in an industry that is difficult to get into, consider job vacancies for positions that you may not ultimately want, including temporary or part-time jobs, as a potential way in. Many employers regularly offer permanent positions to temporary staff when their contracts end. To be realistic, this is unlikely to be the case in a not-for-profit agency, which would probably need to be seen to be fair and open the vacancy for anyone to apply for. However, if you had already gone through the normal recruitment process to secure a temporary contract, covering maternity leave for example, the charity may still legitimately choose to make that contract a permanent one at a later date, particularly if the mother chooses not to return after the end of her maternity leave for example. Do remember, however, that an employer is legally required to give a job back to a mother once she returns from maternity leave, so never count on maternity cover being a guaranteed way into a job. If this is the case, the temporary contract will still place you in a stronger position than if you had not worked for the organisation at all.

Temporary contracts give you:

- Valuable experience working in the industry you want to specialise in.
- Proof to potential employers that you are serious about working in their industry.
- Inside knowledge of any forthcoming permanent vacancies that you may apply for.
- The chance to show your employer that you are worth taking on as a permanent member of staff.

Many organisations use interim managers to fill gaps caused by take-overs, management buy-outs or other major restructures. If you are looking for work at a senior management level, this is a good way of getting into a company. You will be brought in on the understanding that you will be able to turn the business around, or at least hold it together until a permanent appointment can be made. You may be offered a short-term contract of three to six months. However, if things go well, you might find that your contract is extended indefinitely. In addition to being an excellent alternative way of finding a job that may eventually become a permanent position, this type of work also gives you the chance to try out a company and see if you actually like working for it.

> ❝ Work experience is a great way to find out what a company is like and to show your abilities, but competition can be tough. ❞

WORK EXPERIENCE

Work experience is another fantastic way for you to find out what a company is like to work for and for them to see that you are a great candidate to employ. In addition, it also adds an extra dimension to your CV. In some sectors, such as corporate law, accountancy or management consultancy, many firms provide a regular and organised system of work placements, also called vacation schemes and internships. Competition for these can be as tough as for the jobs themselves. To secure a placement, you will need to approach it as seriously as you would a real job application. The application deadline can close many months before the scheme is due to start and some are only available to undergraduates in their penultimate year of study.

Even if the firms you are interested in do not seem to offer organised work placement schemes, it is worth contacting them and offering yourself as an available candidate for work experience. The chances are they would be grateful for an extra pair of hands during times when staff are likely to be on holiday, such as summer or Christmas especially if they are a small company. If you are a student, this should fit in well with your own breaks from studying If you are already employed and want to

 To find out about undergraduate work experience opportunities, contact your university careers office or check out your chosen company's website.

test out a new company or even career, there is no reason why you should not give up some of your annual leave to investigate whether the grass really is greener elsewhere.

Work experience provides you with many of the same opportunities as a temporary job, including the potential offer of a permanent job. It is well worth putting up with the financial hardship of little or no income for a few weeks.

Shell Step

Another excellent source of work experience is Shell Step, which places undergraduates into **SME**s for project-based work. Companies sign up to Shell Step, outlining details of the project they would like a student to complete during a summer work placement and Shell Step links them up with a local student who fits the bill. To qualify, you must be an undergraduate in your second or penultimate year.

Knowledge Transfer Partnership

The Knowledge Transfer Partnership (KTP) is a great way for graduates to secure project-based work experience. Partly funded by the government, it is a programme designed to bring together graduate knowledge and business in order to help businesses improve their competitiveness and productivity through the better use of knowledge, technology and skills.

Recent graduates are invited to work on projects that are often central to a company's strategic development

Jargon buster
SME Small to medium-sized enterprises, typically numbering 1–250 employees

❝ The Knowledge Transfer Partnership brings together graduate knowledge and businesses to improve competitiveness and productivity. ❞

or long-term growth. They are supported by experienced staff from the company, as well as their university, college or research body. The KTP also plays a key role in encouraging dialogue and the transfer of knowledge between businesses and universities.

There are around 400 new vacancies per year covering many subject areas from science and engineering to social sciences. The partnering company, in conjunction with the university or college, undertakes the recruitment for their Partnership. There is no closing date for applications as recruitment of associates takes place throughout the year.

Case Study | Susie

Susie wanted to be a journalist, but rarely found any jobs for first-timers advertised in national newspapers or trade papers such as *Press Gazette*.

In fact, the few vacancies she did find were all for experienced reporters or sub-editors. In need of an income to pay her rent and bills, Susie got a job in a restaurant working as a waitress. As she worked shifts, she found that she could organise her schedule so that she always had one or two days off during the week.

After contacting her local radio station, Susie was given the chance to take up a work experience placement for one day a week in the newsroom. She found her first day terrifying, as she realised that not only did she have no experience as a reporter, she was unfamiliar with the radio station's computer system and knew nothing about the complex digital audio equipment used by the reporters to record interviews, sound bites and reports. She also discovered an entire language that meant nothing to her, such as the word 'slug' that referred to the name of a news story, or 'feed', which means a continuous supply of news coming in from an agency such as IRN.

After six months of work experience, though, Susie was not only proficient in radio terminology and technology, she had also created her own newsreel; a tape of her broadcast work that she could use to support her applications for jobs as a reporter. She had also built up a network of contacts and soon learnt of a job at the independent radio station in her neighbouring town, which she successfully applied for.

VOLUNTARY WORK

Another excellent way to gain valuable work experience and enhance your CV is to do some voluntary work. For some careers, such as medicine, it is difficult to even get a place on a degree course unless you do have some voluntary experience. For a degree in medicine, you would ideally need to have some experience in a caring or health environment, such as a nursing home, local hospice or even a homeless shelter.

Most employers have a very positive view of any candidates who have done some voluntary work. In addition, voluntary work helps you to expand your network of contacts, identify what kind of work you would and would not like to pursue and builds confidence.

One way of finding voluntary work is simply to contact a charity that you are interested in. Most charities rely heavily on the goodwill of voluntary staff and

> ❝ Most employers have a very positive view of candidates who have done some voluntary work. It also helps you to expand your network of contacts. ❞

 For further information on Shell Step and to register, go to www.step.org.uk. For further information about the Knowledge Transfer Partnership, including details on how to apply, see www.ktponline.org.uk or call the helpline 0870 190 2829.

How to find volunteer work

Time Bank A charity dedicated to matching the interests and skills of individuals with volunteering opportunities that suit their lifestyles; see www.timebank.org.uk.

Volunteering England Promotes volunteering in England and runs volunteer centres to help volunteers find appropriate work; see www.volunteering.org.uk.

Voluntary Service Overseas (VSO) Responds to requests from governments and community organisations throughout Asia and Africa with volunteers who work on specific placements; see www.vso.org.uk.

so are delighted to receive offers of help. Depending on their size, some charities have departments devoted to finding suitable openings for volunteers and managing their work. Smaller charities, however, may approach this in a more ad hoc fashion.

Alternatively, you could contact an organisation such as Time Bank, Volunteering England (who match your skills and time to charities throughout the UK) or Voluntary Service Overseas (VSO). VSO recruits volunteers to work on overseas projects, largely in developing countries, with the aim of passing their expertise to local people.

WORKING IN RELATED TRADES

If work experience and voluntary work are not for you and there are no temporary contracts to be found, a good way of getting in to an industry that never seems to have any job vacancies available is to start off with any old job you can get, regardless of whether it is the position you are after or not. The idea is that once you are in, you can get to know the managers of the areas you would like to work for. Perhaps you can offer to do some work for them in your spare time and generally make yourself indispensable until you are able to take an opportunity to make your break.

TV and radio host Jonathan Ross was once voted 'the most powerful man in broadcasting'. He is also one of the most highly paid presenters in the UK. However, he did not begin his career as a broadcaster, he began as a researcher. Some senior newspaper journalists and editors began their working lives as editorial assistants or office secretaries. Many of the general secretaries of the UK's most powerful unions began in jobs represented by their union. For example, general secretary of the Communication Workers Union, Billy Hayes, began his career as a postman. The general secretary of Amicus, Derek Simpson, left school at 15 to take up an apprenticeship in an engineering firm.

It is also worth remembering that your career path may take a route that you had not imagined, or at least had not set out to do. You may also be able to benefit from pragmatic decisions and unforeseen opportunities. Shami Chakrabati is the director of the National Council for Civil Liberties, known as Liberty. She began her career as a barrister. She was called to the Bar in 1994 and worked as a lawyer in the Home Office for five years before joining Liberty as its in-house barrister in 2001. Two years later, she took over as director.

> **"Speculative approaches are a hit-and-miss method, but they might pay off if you show you are right for an upcoming vacancy."**

SPECULATIVE APPROACHES

Another way to secure a job that is not advertised is to apply for one on a speculative basis. There is some debate about the efficacy of this type of approach. You may send out 20 CVs and each one may find itself flying straight into the nearest wastepaper basket. However, if you send a strong covering letter and good CV, a company with an upcoming vacancy may contact you straight away. Equally, a firm that does not have a position available may choose to file your application for later use. A large company may even refer you to a vacancy in a sister location.

Speculative approaches are pretty hit and miss, and success largely depends on the preference of the individual you

contact. So don't automatically assume your CV and letter are poor if this approach doesn't get you very far. It may be that your contact prefers to use an agency or that you are applying at a time when there are no vacancies. Equally, if you phone a company and find that you are rudely rebuffed, try not to take it personally and do not allow it to dent your confidence. You may have just phoned at a bad moment and your stressed contact may have taken it out on you.

As in all job applications, however, there is a good and a bad way to go about doing it. To give your speculative approach the greatest chance of success, follow these rules:

- **Direct your application to a named person.** Call the company and ask to whom you should address an application. If you are automatically put through to that person, don't freeze on the spot but explain that you would like to pursue a career with the firm and ask if you could forward your CV to them. If they say no, you can at least save yourself the trouble.
- **Target your letter and CV** to fit the work of the company. Anything that reads as though it is part of a mass-produced mail shot is likely to fail.
- **Don't make jokes or parody marketing campaigns** in your covering letter. 'Have I got a good deal for you?' probably won't get you very far.
- **Don't ask about salaries or perks.** That is a conversation best left for the end of a second interview.

Creating opportunities

Throughout your working life, you can create future opportunities for yourself by impressing people who may, at some later date, want to employ you.

After being employed for some time, you will discover that the world of work is a small world. Particularly if you work in a niche industry, you will begin to come into contact with the same people. Likewise, you may meet up with former colleagues when you move to a new firm and discover they are there. The first task when it comes to creating opportunities, therefore, is to do a good job in your current position and be recognised by others for having done so. You may impress a client so much, for example, that they offer you a job and try to lure you away from your current position even when you are not looking for a new job.

It is also wise to try to keep conflict with others both within and outside of your company to a minimum. At the very least, you do not want to walk into an interview to find that the person you tipped water over in a fit of pique during a dispute near the water cooler several years ago is now part of the interview panel. If you develop a reputation within your company for being argumentative, it could spread beyond your firm and damage your reputation in your field.

❝ The world of work can be small, and after a while someone might offer you a better position. ❞

PROGRESS REPORT

From the start to the finish of your job-hunting endeavour, it is a really good idea to keep a record of your progress. If you try several avenues, say networking and applying to job advertisements, or you apply for more than one job, everything can begin to blur in your memory and it can be tough to remember who said what and when or if a networked contact returns your call and you haven't the faintest idea who they are and for whom they work. The best thing to do is make

 The world of online networking is burgeoning. To find out more, see pages 56-8.

notes as you go along. These don't need to be particularly detailed. You could record them in a table or on a page that you staple to a copy of whatever application form or CV you have sent.

❝ Don't stick to one route, consider all options and get networking. ❞

What next?

To ensure you find the job you want, you need to look in all of the right places.

1 Check local and national newspapers, the trade press and online job boards (read up on Chapter 3 for a list of the most popular job boards).

2 Get networking (see Chapter 3 for some tips on how to do this online).

3 Visit some careers fairs, careers offices and your local Jobcentre Plus.

4 Analyse the job advertisement carefully and pick out the key words to help you draft your application.

5 Consider work outside your original search criteria, such as work experience, temporary contracts or voluntary work as a good way of entering an industry or strengthening your skills and your CV.

So you have found a job advertisement that you like the sound of – great! But have you looked online? For further details on how the internet can be a great asset in your hunt for a job with online recruitment agencies, job boards and employers' own sites, see Chapter 3.

Going online

In the summer of 2007, a poll by the Association of Graduate Recruiters found that 76.9 per cent of employers will only accept job applications made online. Recruitment agencies, headhunters and applicants all benefit from using online tools in an area that is both increasingly sophisticated and ever changing. To make the most of it, you will need to keep up with the times.

Online technology and you

When it comes to finding the right job for you, the internet is your secret weapon. It is a valuable source of job advertisements, as well as being a great place to find information on the organisations you are interested in. And if you don't head online, you risk missing out on a huge number of vacancies that are only recruited via the internet.

Employers targeting today's under 30s (often referred to as **Generation Y** or the iPod generation) increasingly use sophisticated technology in an attempt to reach them. This can range from text alerts to their mobile phones to **podcasts** offering career advice, online games, blogs and **viral advertising**. Although such methods are less common outside the graduate recruitment sector, what began as a way of reaching the iPod generation

has repercussions throughout every section of today's job marketplace. In particular, there is no ignoring the importance of direct online recruitment.

At the heart of nearly all of today's employment processes lies a company website or possibly a dedicated **microsite**, with an area devoted to attracting top-quality candidates. So, if the last job application you made only involved paper and a pen (and possibly

Jargon buster

Generation Y University-educated first- or second-jobbers often born during the 1980s

Microsite Mini website linked to its parent site, but specialising in a specific area such as recruitment. Microsites often also have their own web address

Podcast Information contained in an audio format that can be played on a mobile device such as an MP3 player or iPod, or through a PC. Some recruiters enable information to be downloaded from their websites via podcasts

RSS Acronym for really simple syndication – a tool that enables people to receive continuous 'feeds' on a particular subject or from a particular source. Subscribers can receive instant alerts to their computers, mobile phones or mobile devices such as BlackBerrys

Viral advertising These are messages or concepts that are compelling enough to make people want to pass them on, often through chatrooms or email messaging

a telephone), you will need to completely rethink your approach to job-hunting. This is not to say that you need to go out and buy an MP3 player to listen to a recruiter's podcasts or a BlackBerry to receive the latest new job RSS feeds while you are out and about, but you will need to go online.

The increasing use of the internet by employers makes good business sense. It can radically reduce the amount of time and money that an employer needs to spend on recruitment. And what employer wouldn't want to cut costs and save time? The saving is often reinvested in slick marketing campaigns that are designed to attract the best candidates. This is important for the large number of employers, particularly those recruiting graduates, that have difficulty in filling vacancies.

Viral advertising

In addition to being slick, many websites also try to be clever and spread their presence through techniques such as viral advertising in an attempt to encourage the spread of word-of-mouth marketing. One such example of this ploy is www.getthemessage.net, a website published by the Royal Navy showing five video scenarios of sailors in action roles who will pass on a top secret message for you via email or mobile phone. The idea is that people will be impressed by what they see, talk about it among their friends (possibly within online chatrooms), and hopefully encourage more people to take an interest in the Navy as a possible career option.

> In 2007 only 68 per cent of the employers that were surveyed by the Association of Graduate Recruiters were able to fill all of their vacancies.

&& It makes good business sense for employers to make more use of the internet. It reduces time and money for the whole recruitment procedure. &&

REVOLUTIONISING RECRUITMENT

Software developed by companies like Skillstream and BackgroundChecking.com mean that with some employers, you can complete every stage of searching and applying for a job online.

The process begins when an employer uses an automated email to send the job advertisement to pre-selected recruitment agencies, potential candidates listed on their database, job boards and their own site.

Your application will then be sifted with pre-programmed search terms and you may also be asked to complete some online tests. Background checks, from Criminal Records Bureau checks to confirmation of basic details such as exam results or references, can also be automatically requested.

If you fail at any of these stages, you may be informed by email or an automatically generated rejection letter. If you get through to the final online stage, you will be invited to interview. If you got down to the final few but are not offered the job, you could be 'kept warm' with the other near-misses in a database, ready to contact next time an appropriate position becomes available.

For any employer that is recruiting several hundred or even scores of new applicants each year, online automation can revolutionise the way that they, and you, work.

alcohol and health screening. The key when applying for any position is, don't lie (see also the box, above).

> **❝ Lying in applications is common, but more employers are checking information now. ❞**

BACKGROUND CHECKS

Employers are increasingly turning to agencies like BackgroundChecking.com to confirm the truthfulness of candidate applications. Details that can be checked include: personal and financial status, criminal record, previous employment experience, education and qualifications, international identity documents, drug,

ONLINE NETWORKING

Online networking operates in much the same way as the offline version (see pages 43–5) with the exception that you can do it within a forum where networking is expected. So, although you may still contact individuals that are unknown to you, it won't be a completely cold call because the person you contact has put him- or herself into an arena where contact is encouraged. Networking sites that are specifically aimed at the professional market, such as LinkedIn, are good for this as members tend to list their job profiles

For further information on Skillstream and BackgroundChecking.com, see www.skillstream.com and www.backgroundchecking.com. See also 'Personal security' on pages 62-4, which explains the potential drawbacks of using the internet.

Most popular social networking sites

Bebo Networking site which hosts blogs, videos, photographs and even author profiles; see www.bebo.com.

Facebook Social networking site used by individuals and companies; see www.facebook.com.

Friends Reunited One of the original social networking sites that began by bringing former schoolmates together and has grown to include dedicated jobs sites, genealogy sites and lonely hearts sites; see www.friendsreunited.com.

LinkedIn Site used by professionals seeking contacts in related industries, job seekers and freelancers; see www.linkedin.com.

MySpace Videos, forums and blogs are available on this site from around the world. The site is used for marketing big names in entertainment as well as profiling unknown talent; see www.myspace.com.

Second Life Virtual reality site, allowing you to move around a virtual world as an avatar, you can swap real money for virtual money so there can be a costly crossover into reality; see www.secondlife.com.

YouTube Video site where members can upload videos for broadcast on almost any topic, which are divided into categories; see www.youtube.com.

and work history on the site. LinkedIn also lists job vacancies (for website information, see the networking sites box, above).

The rules of offline networking apply to the online version in just the same way. They include:

- Keep careful notes, tracking the route through which you came to someone.
- Be polite. Don't be pushy and never ask for a job directly.
- Explain how and why you came to contact a person. For example, you could email, 'I see you are part of the same Facebook network as me and I was interested to read that you work for Essex County Council. I am hoping to move out to Essex from the London Borough of Hackney and wondered what the recruitment conditions are like at Essex. Do you know if there is someone that I might be able to talk to there?'

Social networking sites

Employers also recognise the value of social networking sites. Second Life, a virtual reality world where visitors use **avatars** to interact with one another, has famously hosted virtual job fairs that are attended by technology company IBM, management consultant PA Consulting, and facilities management company Sodexho.

Representatives from the Yellow Pages' online site www.Yell.com have also enjoyed a presence in Second Life as avatars offering information on Yell.com recruiting.

Employers, including accountancy firm Ernst & Young, law firm Linklaters and manufacturer of household brands Unilever, have employers' profiles on Facebook. Future graduate trainees of Linklaters are even encouraged to 'talk' to each other through Facebook so that they have a chance to get to know each other before they take up their positions. PricewaterhouseCoopers runs a video advertisement on YouTube, and many employees from a multitude of organisations list, and even discuss, their employers on sites such as Bebo, MySpace and Friends Reunited.

Before creating your own presence on such a site, think about your 'netrep' and remember that anything you publish online in a public forum can be read by anyone. Do you really want a prospective employer to see you dressed as Harry Potter at a Hallowe'en party, or ranting about how you hate your boss? Although some employers wouldn't search for a potential candidate online, asserting that an individual's personal and professional life has a right to remain separate, most would refuse to interview someone who they know has posted an offensive blog.

CROSSING BORDERS

The internet is an easy way to spread the geographical reach of your job-hunt. Think about your work and your personal life and ask yourself: 'Do I really need to be in the UK?' You are legally allowed to work in any country that makes up the European Economic Area without the need for a work visa. Don't forget that this immediately widens your search area and provides you with many more opportunities to find employment.

Use the internet to search jobs in the EEA and compete on the international stage. Many companies actively try to encourage this and use online recruiting and even telephone interviews to enable potential recruits to progress right to final interview stage without having to spend too much on travel expenses. The same can be said for companies that recruit overseas talent into the UK. Ignoring opportunities in Spain, for example, despite competing against Spanish candidates in the UK, may limit your chances of finding the job you want.

Finding jobs online

There are four main ways you can research and find jobs advertised online: on an employer's own website, in job listings of recruitment agency websites or by signing on as an applicant, and in job boards.

SEARCH AN EMPLOYER'S WEBSITE

If you already know which employer, or group of employers, you would like to work for, check out their websites. It is quite likely that they advertise jobs directly there. How they go about doing this depends on the employer, however.

- Some welcome speculative applications throughout the year and will ask potential applicants to submit a CV regardless of whether they have a specific post available or not.
- Others, especially those that recruit a set number of graduates each year onto trainee programmes, follow a routine and a calendar with a deadline that is about the same date every year.
- Others, particularly those that advertise popular jobs, can suddenly declare that recruiting for a certain job is open and close this window after a short period, such as a week. If your employer falls in the latter category, you'll need to keep an eye on the website and repeatedly check to see if recruiting has opened.

Opening doors to further opportunities

You may know of one or two employers in a particular sector that you are interested in working for, but do you know all of them and do you know about the smaller ones?

The internet also gives you a chance to research the company you are thinking about working for. Some websites, especially those of the big corporations, show what a company's offices look like, often including break areas. Employee blogs offer a sense of what it is like to work for a company and some include video clips of talking heads. All of this helps you build up a picture of what an organisation may be like to work for and whether it is for you. Don't forget, that come application or interview stage, any information that you can learn about a company will help your chances too.

 Information on submitting a CV online is given on pages 108–9. Advice on filling in application forms online is covered on pages 132–5.

A further valuable online source of information includes the archived files of newspaper and magazine stories. Most publications keep an online archive, some of which you may access for free and others that you have to pay for.

"Sign up online to be told news about potential employers. "

Keeping in touch with potential employers

The internet is also a great way to keep in touch with a potential employer. You can use their website to keep up-to-date with developments within the company. Some sites will enable you to sign up to email or RSS alerts, for the company's latest news stories or press releases. Others will simply post developments on their site as they happen and will require you to visit the site from time to time to check on developments.

However, some employers will actively seek to keep a relationship going with you. Perhaps you approached them on a speculative basis and they have asked you to keep in touch as they would be keen to meet you if an appropriate vacancy came up. Others may want to do the same if you were an unsuccessful candidate for one job, but want to keep you in mind for another job. They have to have your permission to do this, but do take such approaches seriously. It is hassle for companies to maintain a database, with physical, technological and legal difficulties. A company would not try to maintain contact with you unless they were genuinely interested. So reply to emails promptly and feel free, if appropriate, to drop your contact an occasional email to note a development you have seen about their organisation or to disclose any development in your own career or education. Remember at all times that this is a professional relationship. Make sure that all of your communication is in well-constructed sentences, never use mobile phone text language and avoid stepping over the line of familiar rather than friendly.

ONLINE RECRUITMENT AGENCIES

In addition to searching the websites of direct employers, you can search the websites of recruitment agencies, both in the UK and internationally. Some recruitment agencies only have an online presence, whereas others also have a high street office that you can visit.

Advantages of using an online agency

- You can contact them at a time and place that is convenient to you. It might be much easier to sign up with an online agency during the evening if you have a job to go to during the day
- Some online agencies, or at least those with a web presence, will post your CV onto a CV database for recruiters to search.
- Geographical location doesn't matter. If you are looking to work overseas, you are more likely to find an agency that can help you online than on the local high street.

Advantages of using a high street agency

- If you use an agency you can visit, you can pop in and build up a rapport with the consultants. Recruitment consultants are paid to fill positions, not find jobs for people, so you are more likely to get them on your side (or at least to remember you) if they have met you.
- If you speak to someone in person, they are more likely to share their knowledge of an industry or prevailing conditions in an informal one-to-one chat than they are online.

Some online recruitment agencies publish job vacancy listings that you may respond to and others prefer to take your details first and match them to their unpublished database of vacancies.

JOB BOARDS

Online job boards are websites that contain lists of job vacancies. There are literally thousands of them available online, both generalist and specialist. Some can be found within the websites of newspapers or recruitment agencies and others exist by themselves. Simply enter your own search terms (salary expectations, job title or location, for example), and let the site provide you with a list of vacancies that you can apply directly to through the site.

- The advantage of using a job board is that it gives you instant access to a wide range of jobs.
- A disadvantage is that if the job has been placed there by a recruitment agency, it is not always possible to find out who the employer is at this stage. In addition, unless you use a portal such as those developed by Innovantage (outlined overleaf), you may need to search many job boards to find what you are looking for.

Popular job boards in the UK

Fish 4 jobs UK-wide job board; see wwwfish4jobs.co.uk.

The Guardian Newspaper classifieds published online are regarded as job boards too; see www.guardianjobs.co.uk.

Job serve The world's first job board, lists UK, US and Australian jobs; see www.jobserve.co.uk.

Local Government Channel For public sector jobs; see www.localgovernmentchannel.com.

Monster One of the world's biggest job boards with a global presence; see www.monster.co.uk.

Prospects For UK graduate jobs; see www.prospects.ac.uk.

Total jobs UK-wide job board that also allows you to upload your CV; see www.totaljobs.com.

> ❝ You'll get more information from a direct, informal chat. ❞

 For more information about working with recruitment consultants, especially an agency that you are dealing with on a face-to-face basis, see pages 138–44.

ONLINE SEARCH TECHNOLOGY

As with everything involving technology, online job searching is an area that is evolving fast. One of the most revolutionary developments entered the recruitment marketplace near the beginning of 2008. The unique technology, developed by the online search company Innovantage, allows job seekers to search vacancies listed on multiple job boards as well as thousands of direct employer websites via a single portal. At the time of its launch, Querki.com (www.querki.com) is the only website that allows job seekers to search for vacancies listed on employers' own sites.

Querki.com is just the latest internet search tool developed by Innovantage. Another one, called Insight, has been operating for over a year. It enables recruitment agencies to search over 400,000 live vacancies advertised on the internet every month. The tool scans the websites of employers as well as job boards and, in addition to compiling the job information, identifies whether an advertisement has been placed by another recruitment agency or not. It also provides recruitment profiles detailing how a given company recruits, what they recruit for, how often and what they pay. General market information on each company, such as their address, sector, number of employees and contact details of key personnel, is also provided.

CV DATABASES

The American-founded jobs website Monster has a worldwide presence. Its UK website holds the nation's largest CV database with well over three million CVs and a reputed 100,000 new ones added each month. You can also upload your CV to the database of some newspapers' websites, including *The Guardian*'s at www.guardianjobs.co.uk, together with the databases of many recruitment agencies.

Most of the CV database sites use CV-uploader software to transfer your CV onto their files. This is relatively easy to use; simply follow the site's instructions. However, don't just upload your paper CV without thinking about the special needs of an online one. These apply to online job applications too (see pages 132–5).

PERSONAL SECURITY

Internet recruitment is not all good news about making life easier for recruiter and applicant alike, however. The technology can only be good if it works properly. In 2006, the NHS suffered from intense embarrassment when it was revealed that the personal details of junior doctors were accessible to the general public through their special recruitment website.

 The website for Monster is www.monster.co.uk. For details of other recruitment agences, see page 214.

The error was quickly rectified, but not quickly enough to deny the fact that a serious breach of security and confidentiality had occurred.

Any agency that uses a database, including recruitment agencies and job boards, is legally required to comply with the Data Protection Act. The Act gives you the right to find out what information is held about you and, among other requirements, puts the onus on the 'data controllers' to ensure the information is kept securely and is processed for limited purposes.

Job board security

If you upload your CV to a job board, you are giving your permission to that job board to hold information about you on their database. You have a right to access it and may request it to be altered or removed from the public domain. Most job boards publish their security policy on their website, detailing how they keep your details secure and the rights you have over them. It is a good idea to read up on this before you upload your CV.

It is also worth remembering that anyone who registers to do so can access your CV via a searchable online database. Before you upload it, therefore, it is a good idea to think about who might read it and what you want them to know about you. For example, is it OK for your current employer to see your posting?

❝ It is vital to keep personal details off the internet. ❞

Do you want your home address and phone number revealed to all?

Some websites allow you to upload your CV so that you can send it to employers. Some allow you to upload it to a searchable database. If you only want to use the former service, make sure the site you use ensures your CV will not be posted online. You should be aware that CVs you complete at your current place of work may be monitored by your current employer!

Safety on the net

To keep yourself safe:

- Remove any personal information such as your address and phone number and avoid including any sensitive information such as your ethnic origin, religious beliefs, political beliefs, physical or mental health and criminal convictions.
- You should also consider your referees. If you plan to upload a CV that contains details of your referees, you will need their consent in writing before you publish it.

A further level of personal security is offered by websites such as Quiet Agent (www.quietagent.com) and Work Haven (www.workhaven.com), which allow you to keep your identity secret until you choose to reveal it.

Some job boards, such as Monster, include additional security 'buffers'. For example, if you have not logged onto their website for 18 months, they will automatically make your CV unsearchable. They also encrypt all information that is sent between your computer and their servers in an attempt to minimise unauthorised third party use, although they cannot guarantee that such information would not be intercepted and unscrambled.

> "The internet is a great job-hunting resource, so hone your research skills and maintain an online presence."

What next?

The internet is a great resource that can help you in your search for a job. The more you use it, the more useful it could be. For example, the more you network online, the greater your online presence will become and the more likely you will come across a strong lead.

1. **Network, search and apply for jobs online.**
2. **Research your prospective employer and remember they can research you.**
3. **Be internet savvy and take care of your netrep and your personal security.**
4. **Concentrate on key search terms if you submit an online CV or application form.**
5. **Keep in touch with potential employers**

So you have explored all your online and offline opportunities, but how should you go about applying for the positions you have found? Your careers adviser told you your CV should be a maximum of two pages, preferably less, but your brother's CV is four pages long and he is always getting great jobs. Who is right? For further information on this and the golden rules of CV writing, see Chapter 4.

CVs and letters

Your CV and covering letter could make or break
your chance to get your dream job. You may be a
wonderful candidate, but something as minor as a
spelling mistake or forgetting to put the dates of your
employment history could result in your application
finding its way directly to the nearest bin. To give
yourself a chance, your CV and covering letter need
to be not only perfect, but carefully
targeted too.

4

The golden rules of a good CV

There is no one right answer when it comes to the question of what makes a perfect CV, but lots of right answers. By their very nature, CVs are incredibly personal. If your CV is going to work for you, it needs to reflect you.

BE DIFFERENT

What is right for one person and their proposed career path could be catastrophically awful for you. A recruiter may be looking for a particular person to round off a team. Your CV (and your covering letter) can tell them a lot about you and whether you are the person for them. Producing a CV copied from someone else runs the risk of being rejected in an instance whereas one that is more personal to you may have been accepted.

It is also worthwhile remembering that recruiters read a lot of CVs. Ten of the same style CV (with a similar format, similar language and similar qualifications), will not catch their eye as clearly as one that is different. The easiest way to stand out from the crowd is to be yourself and show that you are an individual. But remember to illustrate your skills through examples. Many CVs say that the applicant is a team player, self-starter and hard worker. If you can show that you are a team player through playing hockey in a Sunday league or being a member of a successful sales team in your company, you immediately back up your claims and you begin to sound like a real person. If you can show your individuality on your CV, it will inevitably be different from that of everyone else.

PAY CLOSE ATTENTION TO DETAIL

After urging you to be different, it is important to stress that there are also a few rules that should be applied to all CVs. Your first step on the road to writing your perfect CV is to pay close attention to these points:

- Put your name on every page. Recruiters are human too and can mislay or mix up a pile of applications. Named pages will ensure your application can be easily reunited if necessary.

 Examples of well laid out and designed CVs are given throughout this chapter, starting on page 76.

- Unless you are applying for a creative post, or possibly a job where you are working with children, use only white or cream paper.
- Check and double-check all spellings and grammar. Nearly all recruiters say that CVs with spelling mistakes are instantly rejected. Don't let a careless typo get in the way of your career aspirations.
- Follow the instructions of the job advertisements. If it calls for three copies of your CV, remember to send in three.
- Keep a copy of every CV you send out with a note of which company you have sent CVs to. In that way you can arrive at your interview with a spare copy, confident that it is identical to the one you submitted.

Word checker

Does your CV contain any spelling mistakes? Check yours against this list of commonly misspelt CV words.

- **Commission**
- **Computer program as opposed to training programme**
- **Conceive**
- **Definitely**
- **Liaison**
- **Pursue**
- **Receive**
- **Represent**
- **Stationery (meaning pens and paper) as opposed to stationary (meaning standing still)**

WHAT NOT TO DO

In addition to there being a few rules that can be applied to all good CVs, there are also some things that you should never put on a CV.

- Don't submit a joke name email address. If you have one, change it.
- Unless requested to do so (or you are applying for a job as an actor or a model), there is no need to include a photograph.
- Don't put your salary expectations.
- Never put the reason for leaving your previous jobs, or worse, explain why you hated your last employer.
- It used to be the norm to include your age, marital status or nationality on a CV. Today such information is regarded as obsolete. Part of the reason behind this is that such information could be used to discriminate against you on grounds of your gender, age or ethnicity. It also means that CVs are shorter and more punchy.

❝ A CV with a spelling mistake means instant rejection. Keep it short and punchy, and take a spare copy to the interview. ❞

67

TAKE CARE OF PRESENTATION

Bad CVs are not just the ones with spelling mistakes or the ones that complain about previous colleagues. CVs that fail often commit mistakes in presentation or layout. In addition to looking untidy, this means incorrectly ordering lists of information, or failing to account for apparent gaps in employment.

- **Try to use an easy-to-read font.** This means avoiding anything that looks like script or handwriting. But you may also want to consider sticking to a sans serif font. This would include avoiding the overused Times New Roman in favour of a cleaner-looking one such as Helvetica, News Gothic or Franklin Gothic.
- **Present information in bite-sized chunks.** Most research on how long recruiters spend reading a CV agrees that a 10–20 second scan is all that can be expected on the first reading. Your recruiter will look more favourably on your application if they do not need to search for information. Use clear headings and experiment with the use of bold type, underlining and line spaces to divide your CV into manageable sections.

- Order the information on your CV in a sensible way. When listing your employment history, do it in reverse order, putting your current or last job first. When listing your education, unless you are applying for a job straight from school, college or university, be brief. Your employer will not want to know the exact grades of your GCSEs if you got them 20 years ago. Nor will they want a breakdown of all of your degree's modules.
- **Never leave blank spaces.** These instantly send warning signals to recruiters and suggest that you may be hiding something. If you do have something tricky to mention, refer the reader to your covering letter or dismiss it with a short and simple line such as, 'Career break for travelling'.

❝ Use an easy-to-read font, presenting bite-sized chunks of information in a logical order, with no blank spaces. ❞

If there are tricky issues that you need to address, the best place to do this is in your covering letter – this area is examined in more detail later in this chapter on pages 101-7.

KEEP YOUR CV TO AN APPROPRIATE LENGTH

If you bring two or more recruiters together in one room and ask them about how long a CV should be, prepare yourself for a long and possibly heated argument. Some recruiters insist all CVs should be two pages long. This view is echoed by many books and websites offering CV advice, which all urge you to keep your CV to a maximum length of two pages.

However, speak to a management consultant and you may be told that recruiters in that sector would simply not bother to read beyond the first page of a CV. Conversely, recruiters of software developers or specialist contractors would expect a CV to average four pages because they would want to see a summary of the contracts completed during the previous two to five years. A contractor who completes several projects a year would need a few pages in which to list them all.

The answer, therefore, lies in what is normally expected from within a sector. To be sure of getting it right, just ask. A recruiter will probably appreciate the effort you take if you call and explain that you are preparing your CV for the job application and want to know what length of CV is preferred. Alternatively, seek advice from a recruitment agency that specialises in the area of work you are interested in. The one golden rule that applies to all, however, is to be concise. No CV, regardless of whether it is one page or four pages, should contain waffle or superfluous information.

MAKE YOUR PERSONAL PROFILE SHORT

A personal profile on a CV is a short statement, normally about 50 words long, which outlines your main skills and achievements and summarises why you would be a good candidate for the job. For professional positions the accepted practice is to put this into the third person. For other jobs, especially those that do not require such a formal language, such as teaching perhaps, it is quite normal for this to be written in the first person. However, neither rule is set in stone and you can allow personal preference to dictate what you choose to do. Think about your audience, though. If you use the first person when they would normally expect third, do you think they will accept your maverick approach?

Whether you should include a personal statement or not is also open to debate. Many recruiters maintain it helps the recruitment process, providing a 'soundbite' of an individual's capability from which the first round of rejections may be made. Other recruiters believe it does nothing more than add repetitive information to a CV and that by deleting it, you instantly make the CV shorter (something the advocates of single-page CVs promote).

❝ Establish the CV expectations in your sector. Some recruiters expect more information than others. ❞

69

BE PREPARED TO GET REFERENCES

If a job advertisement asks you to include references as a part of your application, the easiest place to put these is on your CV, normally at the end. If references are not specifically requested, however, it is a commonly accepted practice to note on your CV: 'References available on request'.

The only CVs for whom this practice is less common are those of students or recent graduates. If you are a student, it is normal to include two references. One should be a tutor or supervisor who has taught you and the other could be another academic contact or a previous employer.

> ❝ It is only courteous to ask permission of your referee before submitting your CV. ❞

Asking permission of your referees

It is only courteous to do this before you submit your CV. In practice, very few people would refuse to write a reference for you, but your potential referee may be able to warn you of a forthcoming holiday, which might mean he or she would be away at a crucial moment. If your referee is an academic one, it is possible that he or she has to write a lo of references, so give such a referee a prompt sheet listing your projects, or a copy of your CV. This will help him or her (and by extension, you) should your referee be contacted for a reference.

If you are planning a summer of job-hunting in which it is likely that you will send out several applications, explain to your referees that you are planning on applying to several job vacancies and ask your contacts if you could name them as referees on each application.

If you have not included a referee's name on your CV, you do not need to ask permission before submitting your application. After all, your potential employer may not even request a reference. However, if your recruiter contacts you and asks you to submit the name of a possible referee, it is a good idea to explain that you would like to check that it is okay with the individual first. If you are going to do this, it is not a good idea to keep your recruiter waiting for several days. Take action immediately so that you can submit your referee's contact details as soon as possible.

Who should supply your reference?

- University tutor or course supervisor
- Line manager
- Personnel manager
- Director (if working in a small company)
- Friend in responsible position (if a character reference is required).

Approaching potential referees

The way you approach your potential referees will depend on your relationship with them and whether they know that you are applying for a new job or not. If your line manager sits at the next desk over from you and you regularly chat to each other, an informal verbal request is fine. If, however, the most common way of communicating with your potential referee is by email, do so with your reference request. In all instances, in the same way that you might send a prompt sheet or copy of your CV to an academic referee, it is a good idea to do the same with someone who will provide you with a professional reference.

Character references

If you are asked to provide a character reference, any one of your friends or colleagues can write it. Try to ask someone who has a responsible position and discuss the kinds of things that can be included with him or her. For example, the referee should outline how they know you and how they know the points they make about you. For instance, 'I got to know John when I worked with him in his previous position at Unilever. He was an excellent project manager and always

> **66 Preparing a generic CV to be adapted means you can respond quickly. 99**

met deadlines, no matter how tight,' or, 'I went to school with Rupal and have kept in touch with her ever since. She is a conscientious friend, never arriving late and always remembering details such as the birthdays of each of my children.'

CREATE A GENERIC CV

Preparing a good CV and covering letter can be tough and time consuming. And if, after all of your hard work you find that you are not even called for an interview, it can be a demoralising process too. For an easier, shorter and more successful CV writing experience, you will need a few tricks up your sleeve.

Write a CV before you start looking for a job

Admittedly, the next section in this chapter urges you to think carefully about the needs of your recruiter, which makes writing an advance CV a bit tough. However, the first CV you need to write is a generic one that you will never, and in fact must never, send out. Your generic CV will, however, be really useful to you if:

* You have to turn an application around quickly. Most job vacancies have application deadlines, some of which can be pretty tight. If you already have basic details, such as the dates and levels of your qualifications, recorded in a single document, it will only take you a few seconds to copy and paste this into your new CV.
* You also have a ready-written personal statement (about your current position if you have a job or about your

qualities if you don't), you can adapt these to make them relevant to the job application you wish to make.

- You want to apply for more than one position because having a CV ready to copy should save you time and it means that you are less likely to make mistakes too.

For example, look at the sample generic CV for Jane Brown given opposite. When she comes to write an actual job application, she has the salient points at her fingertips even though she would need to expand the sections outlining her career summary and her qualifications, tailoring them to meet the requirements of the job she is applying for.

Have a list of active words to hand

When writing a CV, application form or covering letter, it pays to have a list of active words to hand before you start writing. Positive and action-based words tend to come across better than passive descriptions (see box above, right). This is not to say that you should pack your CV full of elaborate terminology. This could run the risk of appearing to have used a cheap translation computer program to turn your CV into English from a foreign language. However, a phrase like, 'I successfully refocused the marketing strategy' sounds a lot stronger than, 'I worked on the marketing strategy', for example.

Enhance your CV

Here are the top ten active words to include in your CV.

- achieve
- co-ordinate
- enable
- flexible
- initiate
- manage
- organise
- resolve
- successful
- versatile

❝ Positive, action-based words work better than passive descriptions, and beware of using elaborate terminology. **❞**

Sample generic CV for customer service manager

Use this example CV as the basis for yours. The main headings will act as trigger points for composing your own generic CV.

Contact details

Jane Brown

Address, Phone numbers, Email address

Current position

Customer Service Centre manager for XYZ Utility Company, since 2006.

Responsibilities include:

- Managing a team of 30
- Providing 'on-call' advice and support for my team
- Organising professional development and training
- Leading staff appraisals
- Managing the department's budget

Career summary

2001–2006 Assistant Manager, Customer Services, XYZ Utility Company

1999–2001 Supervisor, ABC Telesales

1998–1999 Telesales Executive, ABC Telesales

1992–1998 Sales Assistant, AAA Shoe Store

Education, training and qualifications

2007 – management training

2005 – computer training

2001 – management training

1987–1992 Townville Highschool, 5 GCSEs: English language, mathematics, food science, biology and geography

Additional information

Clean driving licence

Active, enjoy sports, including netball and hockey

Writing your CV

The key to a brilliant CV is to think about the reader. This means working out exactly what your prospective employer wants from a recruit and then showing how you can match that profile.

CONSIDER YOUR AUDIENCE

When it comes to applying for a real job, gather together your generic CV, your list of words, thesaurus or dictionary and then stop and think about who you are going to write your CV for. What do they want to see on your CV? The chances are that they will be looking for a recruit who fits a particular profile.

- Think about how you can fit it.
- Consider how you could enhance that profile even further by highlighting your personal qualities in addition to your work experience.
- Play down or, if possible and without lying, miss out things about yourself that do not fit the profile.

List the qualities and qualifications you feel the job requires

You can also bolster this list with the examples listed in the job advertisement. For example, you may wish to apply to an airline for a position with its cabin crew. Before you write the CV, draw up a list of the things you believe an airline would want from its cabin crew. This may include: amiability and good customer service skills, reliability, punctuality, ability to work shifts and spend several days away from home, fluency in a foreign language and calmness under pressure. The job advertisement may also call for applicant who are friendly and helpful. This list should then comprise the basis of what you write about yourself.

When you describe yourself as a warm, motivated, people-person who prides yourself on your punctuality and is happy to work shifts, you will be far more attractive to your potential employer than if you simply state that you enjoy flying. But remember to give examples. Anyone can describe him- or herself as a people-person, but can you prove it through an anecdote or an award? If you can, your CV will have a greater chance of being noticed.

- If you are not fluent in a foreign language but are keen to improve you language skills and are attending an evening class, say so. Your prospective employer will appreciate your honesty in owning up to potential weakness and may even consider paying for you to attend an intensive language course
- If you have experience in both computer programming and working

as a waiter or waitress in a restaurant, be explicit about the skills you gained in the restaurant, as many of them are directly transferable to those needed by cabin crew. Computer programming is less obviously transferable and, unless you received promotion or rewards for qualities you particularly want to highlight, it is not worth mentioning it in any detail on a CV aimed at a cabin crew job.

INDUSTRY EXPECTATIONS

Always think about the expectations of the industry or sector you want to work in. What the advertising industry considers to be good practice in a CV will be radically different to what an IT company may look for.

IT and technical sector

If you are looking for a job in the IT industry or technical sector, your potential employer will be looking for a CV that quickly tells them that you are qualified and experienced in the area or project that they want you to work on.

- **Put abbreviations** of the industry, recognised qualifications next to your name. These may be Microsoft or Cisco qualifications, for example.
- **After your name and contact details** make a list of your key skills, such as the programming languages you can use and your level of fluency in them.
- **Tell your recruiter** how much hands-on experience you have in these languages or technologies, which ones you have used most recently and

where your strengths lie. Although this gives the recruiter a chance to weed you out more quickly if you are not quite right for a project, it also works in your favour.
- **Don't worry about keeping to two pages.** CVs within this sector, especially for contractors, are regularly as long as four pages.

Experienced IT engineer Sanjay Mukherjee (see sample CV, overleaf) understands that most employers will want to know about his specific technical skills and how experienced he is as a software developer. He ensures that both of these sets of information are given prominence and he therefore places them towards the beginning of his CV. He also knows that the majority of employers who take on temporary contract staff such as himself will want to see what sort of projects he has worked on and the level of his role within each project. In Sanjay's case, this information means that his CV is four pages long. This is normal for his line of work and is what his potential employer will be looking for. For the purposes of this book, however, we end Sanjay's CV after he has listed his first project.

&&In IT or the technical sector, CVs can easily run to four pages because of the level of information employers expect. &&

Sanjay Mukherjee

Address

Phone numbers

Email address

CAREER PROFILE:
- 4+ years of professional experience in .NET Web Development using C#, VB.NET and ASP.NET.
- Excellent team-leading and client-facing capabilities.
- Excellent exposure to complete development cycle.
- Excellent UCD practice and innovative GUI designing with cross-browser support.
- Excellent exposure on .NET WebForm development.

EXPERIENCE SUMMARY: 4+ Years
- Currently working since June 2006 with international management consultant, **BBB London**, as an IT Consultant/Senior Developer.
- Worked for 37 months with **CCC International**, **India**, as a Senior Software Engineer.

ACADEMIC PROFILE:
- BSc in Computer Science, University of Delhi, India.
  April 2003 76% (First Class with Distinction)

TECHNICAL SKILLS:

Languages	C#, VB.NET, C++
Server Scripting	ASP.NET, ASP 3.0
Framework	.NET Framework v1.1 & v2.0
.NET IDE	MS Visual Studio 2003 & 2005
Web Server	IIS 6.0
Web Technologies	Web Services, HTML, DHTML, CSS, XML, Java Script.
Databases	MS SQL 2000
Data Access Model	ADO.NET
Reporting	Crystal Enterprise 10
Object Modelling	UML
IBM Tools	Lotus Notes 6x/5x & Domino – Formula and Lotus Scripts.
GUI Designer	Adobe Dreamweaver
Multimedia	Adobe Photoshop CS

SOFTWARE ENGINEERING METHODOLOGIES:
- Object-orientated.
- Agile software development.
- Waterfall model.

SOFTWARE DEVELOPMENT PHASES INVOLVED:
- Requirements analysis and definition.
- System and software design.
- Implementation.
- Integration and testing.
- Operation and maintenance.

ACHIEVEMENTS:
- Awarded for innovative and efficient solutions.
- Awarded for spontaneous and real-time solution for many production issues.

PROJECTS:

Global People Information

Environment	C#, VB.NET, ASP.NET , Web Services, XML, JavaScript, HTML, Crystal Enterprise 10, .NET v 2.0, MS SQL 2000, MS Visual Studio 2005
Duration	9 months (on-going)
Client	BBB London, UK
Role Played	Senior .NET Lead/Developer
Brief Description	The Global People Information (GPI) Project was established by the HC Executive (HCE) in response to the development of people-based key performance indicators as part of a balanced scorecard approach to monitor the performance and progress of the global firm. It supports the collection of data for the Global Annual Review.

Modules Handled:
Requirements Gathering and Analysis
Design
Implementation
Crystal Enterprise Integration
Unit Testing

Creative and advertising sector

When applying for a job in advertising, regardless of whether it is a creative position or a more managerial one, such as an account handler, you can tear up every CV rulebook you have ever read. Advertising thrives on being individual, eye-catching and memorable. An advertising recruiter will want to see the same principles applied to CVs.

Forget two sides of neatly typed white A4 paper. Anything out of the ordinary would be more welcome. Advertising agencies want employees with ideas and who are strong at lateral thinking. A CV that can demonstrate this would be well received. In advertising, this could well mean an advertisement selling you, of course. But perhaps you could be even more creative and present yourself as a product, with your qualities listed on the packaging. Or maybe you could try a teaser campaign. Whatever you do, make sure it is original.

The same is not entirely true of all creative industries, however. Architecture, interior design and graphic design, for example, tend to be more interested in the portfolio of the architect or designer behind the CV. A strong list of clients with whom you have worked will act as a shorthand for summarising your reliability and quality (you won't have worked with any **blue chip clients** if you weren't good enough), and it is your portfolio that will illustrate your skill. Your potential employer will explain how they wish to see this. They may want you to send in some hard copy examples or photographs of your work along with your CV. They may ask you to email **pdf** examples, or they may prefer to see your CV first and then ask you to bring your portfolio along to an interview or meeting. It goes without saying, however, that a graphic design agency would expect any designers applying for a position to provide a well laid out CV. (For an example of a well laid out CV, see pages 83–5.)

> ❝When applying in advertising, tear up the rulebook and find an approach that shows your strong, creative ideas.❞

Jargon buster

Blue chip company An often large, credit-worthy company whose products or services are well respected and generally successful

Pdf An acronym for portable document format. This is an electronic document or a scan that can contain text or images or both, that must be read with the Adobe Acrobat computer program

Working with children

To be a good teacher, social worker, paediatric nurse or anyone else that works directly with children, you need to be able to engage children.

- **Show that you are child focused.** There are many ways you can approach this. For example, you could present a cover page with a child's drawing of you, complete with quotations from children outlining what they see as your qualities. Maybe you could present your work experience as a timeline, similar to one that you might produce in your history lessons. Or you could list the qualities/skills that you believe a child looks for in you and how you work to obtain those qualities.

- **Illustrate your passion** through anecdotes or examples. Perhaps you recently found an innovative and fun way to help a young child who struggled to understand the concept of simple addition. Showing how you were able to engage the child and find a way in which addition suddenly clicked for him is an excellent way of providing evidence of your approach to teaching. It is also a great way of providing your recruiter with an idea of the person behind the words. To work well with children, you need to be personable. Any evidence you can show of your personality will immediately make your CV appear more appealing.

- **Pay careful attention** to the way you present your personal interests. What you do in your spare time could add great value to a school, ward or day care centre. For example, bringing in your collection of fossils could ignite an interest in prehistory among your children. In this instance you would put on your CV something along the lines of, 'I have an great interest in prehistory and at weekends I enjoy fossil hunting along the Jurassic coast. I would love to bring some of my fossils into school and share my interest with the children.'

In the CV example of a teacher, overleaf, Adam has deliberately chosen a typeface that uses the style of letter 'a' normally used in handwriting. This is to reflect the kind of 'a' that he teaches his children to read and write.

He also shows that he is child focused because he explains that he has encouraged the children in his present class to help with his personal statement.

He then stresses his passion and experience for working with children by demonstrating extra-curricular clubs he is involved with.

 The font used for the CV overleaf was chosen with a specific reason in mind. To remind yourself of the best fonts to use for your CV, see page 68.

Adam Davies

Address

Telephone numbers

Email address

Personal statement

I asked the children in my current Year 2 class to write down what they thought I was like as their teacher without adding their names to the paper. Here is a selection of their comments: Mr Davies has short brown hair. Mr Davies always listens to me. I like Mr Davies because he has a loud voice, especially when he laughs at our jokes. Mr Davies likes trees and football. Mr Davies gave me a hug when I was sad. Mr Davies always reads nice stories.

Employment

September 2005 – current
Butterfly Down Primary School, Yeovil
I currently teach a class of 31 children in Year 2, one of whom has special educational needs. In both 2006 and 2007 my class showed substantial 'value-added' improvements in their SATs. My subject area of responsibility is PE, for which I have a passion both inside and outside of the school. I liaise with the rest of the staff on building the strengths of our PE provision within the curriculum and I run the school's football, netball and rounders clubs. I am also responsible for organising and overseeing educational visits as well as building links with the community. Most recently this included 'Storytime at Primrose View', where supervised groups of children read their favourite stories to some of the residents at our local retirement home. I have planned a return visit next term, where residents will visit the school to read their own favourite stories to the children.

September 2000 – September 2005
Waterfall Infants' School, Truro
As a newly qualified teacher, I was lucky enough to gain experience in both foundation and Key stage 1 at my first school. Between 2000 and 2002 I taught Year 1, 2002 to 2004 I taught Reception and 2004 to 2005 I taught Year 2. This helped broaden my understanding of child development and gave me the opportunity to expand my teaching techniques and tools. I believe I learnt as much from my children as I taught them.

Teaching experience as an undergraduate

Final year teaching practice, 10 weeks, Hillside Primary School, Bath, Year 2.
Third year teaching practice, 12 weeks, Hilltop C of E Infants' School, Bath, Year 1.
First year teaching practice, 10 weeks, Underhill Primary School, Bristol Reception.

Education

2000 BA (Hons) 2:1 Primary Education, University of the West of England, Bristol

1997 'A' levels: English (A), History (B), French (C), Sunnyside Sixthform College, Exeter

1995 GCSEs: English (A), Mathematics (B), Art (B), French (B), Biology (C), History (C), Geography (C), Science (C), Sunnyside School, Exeter

Personal interests

I love playing sport and encouraging other to do so. I play for a Yeovil football club and take part in triathlons when I can. In 2006 I founded Active Kids Yeovil (AKY), a council-sponsored holiday sports scheme for children. The scheme offers subsidised access to a range of sports activities for children during the summer holidays. Activities range from football to archery and the scheme also features Superstar Days, where leading figures in individual sports take part with the children.

References available on request.

Senior executive

When it comes to articulating your CV as a senior executive, it is important to place your achievements in context. They can then be properly understood and appreciated. If your division experienced year-on-year growth under your leadership, put this first. If you received back-to-back promotions in recognition of your skill and talent, make sure you give this fact its due prominence. If you were given special responsibilities, spell them out.

Carys Williams (see CV opposite) has enjoyed a long and successful career as a senior manager in blue chip corporations. She relishes a challenge and knows that with her experience and strong leadership qualities she is well placed to find 'turnaround' work as an interim manager. In such cases, the interim manager works as a troubleshooter, identifying weak spots in the business and taking action to make drastic improvements.

Interim managers are normally brought in to manage a company on a temporary basis. The role could be to manage a specific project, to provide cover for the secondment or maternity leave of the current manager or director, or to manage the company following the departure of the director before a permanent appointment can be made.

In some instances (most commonly where the managing director has left), companies requiring an interim manager may be suffering from a period of unprofitability. Interim managers may use such a temporary position, often six months to a year, to build relationships that lead to permanent positions. However, many interim managers also like to make a career out of turning the fortunes of companies around and do not seek permanent positions at all.

After a long and steady career in senior management, Carys is drawn to the thrill of troubleshooting. She knows that her next employer will be looking for an executive with a strong management track record in a profitable company. To this end, Carys begins with a summary of her current employer in addition to her current role. She then goes on to outline her suitability for her future position by illustrating her key achievements.

> **❝ If your division achieved significant growth under your leadership, put this first, and give prominence to any rapid promotions. ❞**

CARYS WILLIAMS

Address

Telephone numbers

Email address

PROFILE

An effective Operations Director with proven business success and diverse technical ability gained through a range of senior management experience. A good track record of developing strong working relationships with board level executives from a wide range of industries including financial services, publishing, retail and the public sector. Decisive, cost-effective solutions met business needs efficiently and speedily. Now looking for an interim opportunity where these skills can produce targeted, fast, value-added results.

Key achievements

- Recognised as business-oriented technical expert by operational senior management and executive peers.
- Developed new management team with focus on delivering business benefits during transition.
- Devised successful marketing campaign which resulted in a 20% increase in response and increased revenue of £7,000 per month.
- Created a programme of efficiency projects which saved the company over £8,000 per month and equated to 12% of the company's cost base.

CAREER HISTORY

OPERATIONS DIRECTOR, BRAZIERS (UK) LTD
(April 2004–date)

Braziers (UK) Ltd was formed in 2004 as a result of the successful integration of Williams Ltd and Brathwaites. Following the merger, the shareholders invited me to join the firm as Operations Director. Braziers (UK) Ltd provides magazines targeted at the business sector. Post merger we became the third largest business magazine publisher in the UK, with a turnover of around £17m and over 200 staff.

Key responsibilities & achievements
- Delivering year on year growth in line with budgets.
- Developing and managing an effective Senior Management team.
- Sourcing new and profitable revenue streams.
- Developing excellent relationships throughout the industry.

**SENIOR MANAGEMENT CONSULTANT, CARWELLS
MANAGEMENT CONSULTANTS LTD
(January 1997–March 2004)**

As Senior Management Consultant for Carwells, I managed several high-profile projects, including:
- Business process review for the ABC Licensing Agency.
- Finance system implementation for XYZ (a global advertising agency).
- Project to merge HairuLike and BeautyProductsRUs, two mail-order businesses.

One of the largest projects I managed involved reviewing the capabilities of one of Marley Publishing's subsidiary companies. The company was failing to meet expectations and the parent company were considering various options, including merging with a similar-sized business. My work included devising a new corporate strategy and reviewing the organisation's structure, all of its in-bound and out-bound operations, IT, telephony, premises, finance, client management and HR. This resulted in 27 separate change management projects and an overall programme budget of £1.8m.

Projects set up during the process:
- To review the capabilities of the two businesses and prepare a strategy to merge.
- Present findings to the Boards and obtain agreement for Joint Venture Company.
- Review of the technical infrastructure and key software applications at each business.
- Develop initial structure of the new company and assist in appointing an interim chairman.
- Manage press and staff communications.

CARYS WILLIAMS (continued)

CHANGE MANAGER, WATER UTILITY I.S. & BUSINESS CHANGE
(January 1994–March 1997)

Water Utility is the water division of Wet Springs Group and is one of the largest water businesses in the UK with about 12 million domestic and business customers across the north of England.

■ Change Consultancy Team Manager. Managed Water Utility's internal change consultancy team of 16 consultants. Primarily coached and supported the team of consultants across all company business change projects concerning process redesign and the introduction of IT while working on projects myself.

■ Offshore Outsourcing Project Manager. End-to-end project where managed a highly controversial business process outsourcing of 80 'seats' to Indonesian offshore capability to save £1.4m of operating costs over 2 years, without redundancies. The project was the first offshore outsourcing project in the world in the utilities industry.

■ Project Development Manager. Worked with Customer Service management team to devise Change Programme for customer services and associated IT projects. Transitioned a team of six to become internal consultants capable of developing manager's solutions and creating business cases to improve service and reduce costs.

■ Business Change Manager. Responsible for managing business change element of £17.5m project to implement process-led customer system. Used introduction of new system and management information to change behaviours across contact centre.

PROFESSIONAL MEMBERSHIPS

Member of the Institute of Management Consultants
Member of the Institute of Direct Marketing

EDUCATION

MBA	Open University 1998
University of Leeds	BSc(Hons) Managerial Sciences 2:1
Coventry School, Bablake	4 'A' levels and 8 'O' levels

CARYS WILLIAMS (continued)

Special challenges

Some CVs are trickier to write than others. How do you write about your previous employment if you are looking for your first job? And what do you do if you have lots of employment gaps, due to periods of ill health, time off caring for others or a spell in prison?

If your employment history is chequered or even non-existent, the challenges you may face when it comes to writing a CV may be a bit tougher than simply tailoring your approach to the job description and industry expectations. If you find yourself in one of these situations, although your CV will be harder to write, the challenge is not insurmountable. In fact, if you approach your CV in an imaginative and positive way, you may find you come across better than other, blander CVs. This could, in turn, place you in a much stronger position than an applicant whose employment history is more straightforward.

FIRST JOBS

If you are looking for your first job and have no work experience to include on your CV, don't despair or hand in a CV that only takes up half a side of one A4 sheet. Employers do take on first-timers.

Keep skills relevant

All employers want to see is that you have the relevant qualifications and some indication of employability. This means possessing skills that can be used in the workplace. These can be gained anywhere and do not need to have come from your experience in a job. For example, you may have been a volunteer leader at your local community youth club. This would look good on any CV aiming for a job with children or that requires team leadership. You may have taken part in the Duke of Edinburgh Award Scheme. If you have, don't just list it, but say what level of the Award you received and what you did specifically. Most employers will have heard of the Award, but may not know exactly what it entails. Outline what aspects of the programme you took part in and explain how this is relevant to the position you are applying for.

There are some industries that are incredibly difficult to start off in. Information Technology is one. Technology can move forward at such a fast pace that many employers tend to look for coders or programmers with up-to-date project-based experience in specific computer languages and techniques. An educational environment may not supply exactly what they are looking for. That said, however, the industry would collapse if new people never entered it. Your best bet, regardless of the industry you want to work in, is to look for entry-level jobs and training schemes. If none of these appear to be available, keep plugging away. If your CV is repeatedly rejected, be brave and ask for feedback. Is the only reason for your rejection because you don't have enough experience? Ask your recruiter whether the firm ever employs school or college leavers and, if so, how they gained the right levels of experience. Did they have part-time jobs while studying, for example?

Planning your first-ever CV

There are two main points to consider when planning your first CV:

- **Put your education first** and your employment history second. If this is for your first 'career' job after school or college, your employment history is likely to include part-time, low-skilled jobs. Although this is something that a recruiter may be interested in, unless you have already worked in an area that directly relates to your career aspirations, your previous work experience is probably not as important as your education. For example, if you want to apply for a graduate trainee scheme with a law firm, your recruiter will want to see your academic achievements before learning of your holiday job at your local supermarket. However, the reverse may be true if you wanted to apply for a journalism trainee scheme with the BBC and had worked every weekend for the previous year at your local radio station.

- **Ask your careers' office for help** in preparing your CV. Some universities also include CV-writing advice in the careers section of their websites. You may find this useful even if you have not attended the university. A further great source of CV advice for students and graduates is the website Prospects (see the box at the top of page 92). And although it describes itself as 'the UK's official graduate careers website', the information it provides on CVs applies equally well to school leavers as it does to graduates.

In our example CV from a school leaver (see overleaf), James Jones compensates for his lack of employment history by describing his work experience. In addition to the skills gained from the actual experience itself, this also demonstrates that James has the initiative to seek out work experience. With this CV, James is applying for a part-time job that he can do while he finishes his A levels.

On pages 90–1 there is an example of a graduate CV. Iona is able to demonstrate more experience than James. This is because she is older and has had more time to gain experience. Iona's biggest strength is her language proficiency. She is applying for a position on a graduate trainee scheme with a large retailer. She knows that the retailer imports many goods from Italy and she is hoping that her fluency in Italian will help her application. To this end, she stresses it in her personal profile, as well as listing it among her key skills.

James Jones
Address
Telephone numbers
Email address

PERSONAL STATEMENT

I want to make my mark as a businessman, but know that I have a lot to learn first. Although I plan to study business and finance at university after completing my A levels, I know it is important to learn the trade from real business people and work my way up. I am conscientious, hard working and eager to learn.

KEY ACHIEVEMENTS

- City Academy Certificate (Learning Hero)
- Food Hygiene Certificate
- I achieved a place on the "Access to Bristol" course at the University of Bristol (2006)

EDUCATION

City Academy Bristol, 2001 to present
Cabot Primary School, 1999 to 2001

Qualifications
GCSEs:
Mathematics A; English Language C; English Literature A;
Double Science AA; Religious Education A; Art B;
Health and Social Care AA; Statistics C; Citizenship B; ICT Distinction

Predicted grades at A Level:
Mathematics B; ICT B; Business B; Certificate in Financial Studies Merit;
BTEC Finance Merit

WORK EXPERIENCE
Bristol Royal Infirmary
May 2005 Information Provider
As an information provider I was constantly communicating with the public, fulfilling requests such as ward directions and also providing some information regarding patients where appropriate. Working with such a diverse range of people was enjoyable and certainly improved my communication skills.

HOBBIES AND INTERESTS
My hobbies are playing badminton and tennis which I play at home and in the after-school clubs. I am interested in art and enjoy visiting art galleries to compare the work of different artists. I also enjoy travelling to experience different cultures.

REFEREES

Mr C Smith	Mrs B Ahuja
Head of Business Studies	Head of Communications
City Academy Bristol	Bristol Royal Infirmary
Address	Address
Email address	Email address
Telephone number	Telephone number

CV example: graduate

IONA SCOTT

Address
Telephone numbers
Email address

Personal profile

A confident, hard-working graduate who during her Eramus year abroad became fluent in Italian and learnt to work effectively with people from a broad range of cultural backgrounds. A self-motivated team player who has demonstrable leadership skills and who is now looking for an opportunity to actively contribute to ABC Company and develop her career potential.

Key skills

- Leadership qualities – Air Training Corps Senior Cadet/NCO grade, responsible for instructing junior cadets
- Language skills – fluent Italian; good French and German; conversational Spanish
- Teaching experience – qualified Amateur Swimming Association Assistant Swimming Teacher and lifeguard
- IT skills – MS Word, MS Excel, MS Office, MS PowerPoint, MS MapPoint, MapInfo Corporation, MapInfo 8
- Communication skills – customer service experience during vacation jobs at J Sainsbury plc

Education and qualifications

2002--2006 **University of Leeds BA (Hons) Geography-Italian (2:1)**
An investigation of the human aspects of geography including advanced retail planning and geographies of production and consumption, demographics, current affairs, politics and cultural geography.

2004–2005 **Università degli Studi di Ferrara, Italy**
Eramus year. Full year spent in Ferrara as part of degree course.

2004 **Università per Stranieri di Perugia, Italy**
Eramus intensive language course. Two months spent in Perugia, the first at a university specifically for foreigners.

2002–2004 **Peter Symonds College, Winchester, Hampshire**
A Level: French (B) German (B) Geography (B)
AS Level: General Studies (C)

1997–2002 **Kings School, Winchester, Hampshire**
9 GCSEs – 5 x A*, 2 x A, 2 x B

Interests and achievements

- Duke of Edinburgh Award scheme – Silver Award
- Sporting interests – Vice Captain of University basketball team; school hockey; swimming; cross country and basketball teams

Work experience

2005 **J Sainsbury Plc, Olivers Battery, Winchester – Beer, Wine & Spirit Assistant**
Vacation employment. Duties included customer-facing duties requiring basic knowledge of the products.

2000–2003 **Winchester Sport and Recreation Limited – Lifeguard and Swimming Teacher**
Part-time employment. Duties included acting as lifeguard, reception duties, cleaning and general maintenance, swimming teacher.

2001 **Conceria Ambra Srl, Almisano di Lonigo, Italy (one of the largest tanneries in Europe exporting leather worldwide) – Sales Office Assistant**
Work experience placement. Duties included: general office duties, interpreting and telephone answering.

Referees

Academic:

Name

Position

Address

Telephone number

Professional:

Name

Position

Address

Telephone number

EMPLOYMENT GAPS

The first question any recruiter will ask in a chronologically ordered CV that has a gap or gaps is, 'Why is there something missing?' And if there is no good explanation, the second will be, 'If this applicant has already spent a year off work, is this going to happen again and will I need to spend more money and time on recruitment two months down the line?' This will instantly begin to send shivers down the spine of any potential employer and many will simply use this as an excuse to weed your CV out of the pile. Before you know it, and possibly before your qualities have even been noted, your CV will be in the out box, inscribed 'rejection' with an HB pencil. The key, therefore, is to make your recruiter recognise your positive qualities before they panic about perceived potential problems.

How to present a non-chronological CV

This is the easiest way to deal with the problem and is applicable regardless of whether you have spent time away from

The best way to present a non-chronological CV

- List your work experience, along with your employers, under a heading marked 'Skills and Achievements'.
- Put your skills in order of importance, rather than putting your most recent job first and then listing your previous roles in reverse order.

- Although you can put dates on your CV, not having them in order will help to lessen the impact of the gaps.
- Alternatively, simply put the year in which you gained the experience. This will help mask the presence of gaps – an issue you can discuss in more detail in your interview or your covering letter if necessary.

employment caring for children or other dependents, unable to find work after redundancy, through ill health or serving a prison sentence.

Temporary work

If you've been in temporary work, remember that all work experience, including temporary work, is regarded as a positive thing by employers. Don't be concerned about employment gaps when listing temporary work on your CV, these are normal and most employers will not be alarmed by them. Simply put the phrase 'temporary contract' next to the dates that you worked on a temporary job.

Ex-offender

Finding work after a spell in prison can be difficult, but it is not impossible. Try to not let your past get in the way of your future and concentrate on what you can offer your potential employer.

It is probably best to leave your prison sentence off your CV, but it is a good idea to mention it in the covering letter. This will give you the opportunity to explain yourself and will mean that the subject is already out in the open and not something that you have to dread disclosing in the interview. You can find examples of how to write effective covering letters later in this chapter.

In the CV of an ex-offender (see example CV, overleaf), Karl is applying for a marketing position in a small company. He hopes to be able to start work as soon as he is released, so begins sending out job applications while he is still inside. In an effort to avoid alienating his prospective employer from the outset, Karl gives his parents' home address. His parents agree to monitor his mail for him and alert him to any job application response that is sent there. Although he knows that he may have to disclose his period in prison, he wishes to downplay the experience and chooses to present a non-chronological CV to emphasise his strengths.

Dismissed employee

Writing a new CV after having been sacked should not be all that different from writing any other CV. Most employers do not expect to see a column outlining reasons for leaving previous employment on a CV, so you do not have to worry about it here. The tricky part is how to reveal your dismissal and defend yourself in your covering letter. We shall examine how you can do this later in this chapter.

> **❝All experience, including temporary work, is regarded as a positive by employers.❞**

If you are an ex-offender, there is additional information on looking for work after release from prison on pages 30-2. Dismissed employees should see the text on pages 27-8.

Karl Smith

Home address *(don't put your prison address here)*
Home telephone number
Email address *(if you have one, don't worry if you do not)*

Personal statement

Confident, ambitious and hard working, I am reliable and able to work on my own initiative or as part of a team. I get on well with people of all ages and backgrounds. I am self-motivated and am willing to undertake any training required by the company.

Key skills

Team leading and events organisation

As part of a team of volunteers, I worked with adults with learning difficulties, organising a variety of sporting activities and competitions. I assisted with outings that included horse riding, sailing and bowling.

Marketing

I have recently completed a distance-learning certificate in marketing.

Customer services

A people person, I am excellent at dealing with customer enquiries both in person and on the telephone. Experience gained at SS IT Services, Croydon in 1999 and QQQ Data Solutions, Croydon in 1997.

People skills

Since 2007, I have worked at the Adult Day Centre in Woking, organising activities for adults with learning difficulties.

Computer skills

City & Guilds level 3 IT, Windows 95/98, Excel, Word, database management and data-inputting.

Office administration

Banking cheques, managing petty cash, verifying order books, managing office staff. Experience gained at RRR Technical Services, Croydon in 2004 and SSS IT Services, Croydon in 1999.

Karl Smith (continued)

....

Education

September 2002 to date Woking College, City & Guilds Level 3 Certificate in Information Technology

October 2001–September 2002 National Distance College, Distance Learning Certificate in Marketing

September 1998–June 2001 Community College, Croydon, BTEC National Diploma in Business and Finance (passed with merits and distinction)

1992–1997 Croydon Secondary School GCSEs History (B); Maths (B); English (B)

Other qualifications: Windows 95/98 environment, Excel spreadsheet, Microsoft Word.

....

Professional membership

Student membership: Chartered Institute of Marketing

....

Interests

I enjoy listening to music, reading, swimming, socialising and meeting new people. I am also keen on studying to further my career. My aim is to become a full member of the Chartered Institute of Marketing.

....

Referees

Available on request.

PARENTS AND CARERS RETURNING TO WORK

If you have spent several years away from employment while you bring up your children or care for a relative, the work history section of your CV may look quite outdated. However, just because you have not been paid for your work by an employer does not mean to say that you have not been working. The reality is that you have probably worked a great deal harder than an ordinary nine-to-five worker who has no other commitments. By adding this to your CV, you are showing that you did not sit at home twiddling your thumbs for several years.

66 Make the most of the skills and qualities that you showed during any time out of employment, such as caring for children or a relative. 99

Highlight your skills and qualities

The way to make your CV sing is to highlight the skills and qualities you practised or gained during your time as a carer. Don't just make do with a throwaway line such as, 'Cared for my children until they began school', or, 'Nursed my mother during her final years with cancer'. Skills to include might be:

- Time management (organising a school run)
- Dispute resolution (smoothing disagreements between warring siblings)
- Record keeping (monitoring medication for ill dependant)
- Accounts management (running the bank accounts of an ill or elderly dependant)
- Team management (running local toddler group).

Joan Pearson (see example CV, overleaf) took a long career break to care for her ill father. Rather than try to hide it or apologise for it, Joan focuses on the skills she acquired during that period and shows how they can apply to the personnel and project management position she is applying for.

THE LONG-TERM UNEMPLOYED

Just like the CV of a parent or carer who wants to return to work after a long period away, if you have been unemployed for a while, your CV may look outdated if you leave a gap between the date you last worked and now. Try to fill this space with activities, training or work experience that show, despite being unemployed, you are active and relevant to today's market.

CAN'T WRITE, WON'T WRITE

If putting pen to paper in an attempt to sell yourself sounds like too much, you don't have to write a CV at all. The latest

American vogue to hit the UK's shores is that of the video CV. And if talking to a camera is not your thing, you can still dodge the CV writing chore by employing a professional CV writer or agency to do one for you.

Professional CV-writing services

Type the letters 'CV' into any online search engine and you will be presented with thousands of results. Many pages which will be packed with individual writers and agencies offering to write your CV for you. Prices range from around £10 for downloading a CV or CV template that you can copy, to several hundred pounds for a CV that is written specifically for you. Some agencies offer a free CV review, where your current CV is critiqued. Others provide this service for a fee.

Are these agencies worth it? Perhaps. They are not offering anything that you cannot do yourself, and they probably wouldn't save you much time either, as you would still have to provide them with all of the information that you would need to gather when writing your own CV. However, if you feel anxious about writing your own CV or have received rejection after rejection and would like guidance, a CV-writing service may be perfect for you.

The hard part is finding the right agency or writer. Some are inevitably going to be better than others. But most are reluctant to show any examples for fear that people will just copy the examples for free and not pay to have a CV written for them.

- Ask for CV examples directly or to be provided with references from previous customers. (If you show a genuine interest, they may be more willing to show you an example of a CV.)
- You could also ask them to critique your existing CV. If their comments make sense to you, it might be worth signing up to their CV-writing service. If not, shop around a bit more until you find someone who seems to understand you and your needs.

Some agencies also provide guarantees, either offering to continue rewriting your CV until you are happy with it or giving your money back if you wish to cancel.

❝ CV-writing services don't offer anything you can't do yourself, but the guidance could be valuable to you. ❞

Some examples of CV agencies are Accendo CV (www.accendocv.co.uk); Bradley CVs (www.bradleycvs.co.uk); CV 4 You (www.cv4you.com) and the CV Centre Ltd (www.cvcl.co.uk).

Joan Pearson

Address
Telephone numbers
Email address

PERSONAL PROFILE

A highly motivated, skilled and professional project manager, with both generalist skills and specialisms in change management and selection. Now looking for an opportunity to develop a career with a progressive company.

KEY SKILLS

- Excellent communication and interpersonal skills, confident and experienced at working with senior management and with union representatives.
- Commercially perceptive with strong problem-solving skills. Excellent planning and implementation skills.
- Effective decision maker.
- Highly organised and compassionate, able to manage the full-time care of a severely ill dependant.

CAREER HISTORY

January 2001 to date, Career break
Full-time carer for ill father
Providing 24-hour care for my elderly father, who was suffering from severe Alzheimers. Role included:

- Liaison with health care providers
- Administering and recording of medication
- Power of Attorney responsibilities, including the disposal of assets
- Co-ordination of respite care rota.

September 1994 – January 2001 Big Company Plc, Bristol
Senior Project Manager Customer Services (part-time)
Providing a full proactive project management for line managers and staff, including delivery of assessment centres.

- Completed Hay job evaluation and full re-structure of the finance department
- Production and verification of management statistical information
- Ran many individually tailored training courses including a number of 'Managing Under Performance' workshops, which resulted in significantly fewer line manager queries
- Instrumental in a number of change initiatives resulting in savings in excess of £250,000
- Led process re-engineering project groups then devised, implemented and monitored action plans.

Career History (continued)

May 1993 – September 1994, University of Bigtown
Personnel Officer
Providing full personnel and training service to academics and staff, on areas such as:
- Discipline and grievance
- Pay and conditions
- Training and development requirements
- Recruitment and selection
- Policies and procedures.

September 1978 – May 1993
Working for various blue chip companies as a Personnel and Training Officer, including working for Smith Bank plc for 8 years and PPP Motoring Services for 4 years.

OTHER RELEVANT SKILLS

Saville & Holdsworth Level 2-Licensed Assessor
Psychometric Testing, Occupational Personality Questionnaires, Assessment Centre
Design and Evaluation (All Saville & Holdsworth – SHL)
Hay Job Evaluation
IT Literate – email, WP, spreadsheets
EFQM Qualified Assessor

EDUCATION

1973 – 1978   Colstons' Girls School, BRISTOL

QUALIFICATIONS

Certificate Institute of Personnel Development
Certificate Institute of Training and Development AMITD
Institute of Banking Examinations (accountancy, law relating to banking, economics and
finance of foreign trade)
City and Guilds Youth Trainers Award
9 'O' Levels including Maths and English
ONC Business Studies

REFEREES
Available on request.

Video CVs

Video CVs are called showreels in the entertainment industry and, as such, have been around for years. A newer trend, however, is for video or (more often DVD) CVs to be used by other industries. Some, such as advertising and PR, seem to welcome the introduction of videos as alternatives to written CVs. However, this is not true for all industries. A recruiter may take seconds to scan a written CV, but may have to spend at least two minutes on every video. Logistics alone may mean that video CVs may not find themselves popular with every employer.

If you want to create your own video CV, your level of creativity will dictate its form. If you are super-arty, you may be able to produce an animated CV. A simpler approach is to sit in front of the camera and provide a mini-presentation of your achievements, interspersed with footage to illustrate what you are saying. The upside of submitting a video CV is that your recruiter can see how good you are at presenting yourself. This can be a real plus in a customer-facing industry. The downside is that if your TV production skills are poor, you may come across badly even if you would have otherwise been a strong candidate.

One way around the problem of producing a professional-looking video CV is to employ an agency to create on for you. This can be anything from a web-based service that uses a web cam to record your presentation to a studio complete with CV re-writing services.

> **" Video CVs can show off your presentation abilities, but poor production skills could hold back an otherwise strong candidate. "**

 Some examples of video CV agencies are D 7 Recruitment (www.d7recruitment.co.uk); Digital Video Interview (www.digitalvideointerview.co.uk); Purple Web IT (www.purplewebit.com) and Talking CV (www.talkingcv.com).

The covering letter

It is arguable that your covering letter is even more important than your CV or application form. It allows you to express your personality more clearly and gives you the opportunity to defend yourself and emphasise your strengths if your application is weak in any area.

Less rigidly structured than a CV and far more personable than an application form, your covering letter gives you a wonderful opportunity to connect with your recruiter and come across as a real live, thinking, feeling person. This is a quality that can be lost in the more formulaic and list-driven text of a CV. Recognising this, recruiters pay careful attention to covering letters and so should you.

Ten rules of a good covering letter

1 Always address your letter to a named person, even if you have to ring the recruiter to find out his or her name.
2 Give your letter a title and a job reference number where appropriate.
3 Never use a generic letter for all applications. Writing 'I would like to apply for the position of ____ ' and filling the blank with the position named in handwriting is a big no no.
4 Take care when you cut and paste. JP Morgan won't be impressed if your letter is still addressed to Accenture.
5 Keep it short with just one or two examples of your philosophy or approach to work. Your letter should take up less than one side of A4 paper.
6 Check and double-check every line. Typos in your covering letter will have the same disastrous effect on your employment chances as errors in your CV or application form.
7 Always use good quality paper (100 gram) and envelopes. If you have headed paper then you could use this. Do not fold your letter and CV or application form.
8 Check the postage. The Post Office charges letters by both size and weight. The last thing you want is for your prospective employer to have to pay an excess postage fee for your application.
9 Avoid repeating information that you include in your CV or application form.
10 Obey instructions. If you are asked to submit a handwritten letter, or three copies of your CV, do so.

BASIC COVERING LETTER

In a basic covering letter, you only need three paragraphs to say three things:

- Here is my CV.
- The reason I'll be great at this job is because ...
- I'd be happy to meet you at your convenience.

The second paragraph is the most important. Fill your second paragraph with an anecdote illustrating why you are made for the job so that you stand out from every other letter, particularly the ones that just say, 'I am applying for the position of cabin crew. I enclose my CV as requested. I look forward to hearing from you.' For an example of a basic covering letter responding to a job advertisement, see opposite.

DEALING WITH DISCLOSURE

A covering letter also gives you the opportunity to do far more than explain that you are sending in a job application. It enables you to disclose any sticky problems in your work history before you are put on the spot in an interview. In addition, if you have any special requests that need to be accommodated for an interview (if you require wheelchair access or would like your interviewer to know in advance that you have a hearing impairment, for example), your covering letter provides you with a platform from which you can exercise your rights and ask for what you need.

Dismissed employee

If you have been sacked from your last job, you will need to mention it in your covering letter. It would be a disaster for you if the first your potential employer heard of it was from your previous employer. If you were dismissed during your probationary period, however, you can get away with an explanation that is 'softer' than if you were sacked for gross misconduct two years into your job (see the sample letters on pages 104 and 105).

Accommodating specific needs

Of course, not all disclosure letters need to reveal negative things. Your covering letter may just need to ask your recruiter to prepare for your needs during an interview. In the example of Sarah's letter (see page 107) this is to accommodate her hearing impairment. You legally do not have to reveal a disability to a prospective employer at this stage and some people feel that it may affect their chances of success. However, the more notice an employer has, the more chance they have to accommodate your needs adequately.

> **❝ The covering letter is an opportunity to disclose any problems before you are put on the spot at an interview. ❞**

Lincoln Ojolo
Address
Telephone numbers
Email address

Sandra Hall
Job title
Name of organisation
Address of organisation

Today's date

Re: *Cabin Crew Vacancy – Job ref CC101*

Dear Ms Hall

Please find enclosed my CV in support of my application for the position of Cabin Crew with High Flyers Airline.

I am a warm, motivated, people-person and pride myself on punctuality and going that extra mile to keep my customers happy. For example, if a diner in the restaurant where I work has enjoyed a bottle of wine, I will steam off the bottle's label and stick it to a sheet of the restaurant's headed paper. I think this acts as a lovely souvenir of an evening out, as well as providing the diner with a record of the wine should they wish to buy any bottles at a later date. Working as cabin crew would enable me to further my skills in customer care. I want to develop a career with a great company and I have been impressed with the quality service awards High Flyers has recently won. Working with you would give me the opportunity to remain free of the 9–5 grind of many careers as I much prefer working irregular hours or shifts.

I would welcome the opportunity to meet you to discuss how my experience and achievements may meet your requirements and to explore how I may be beneficial to your company.

Yours sincerely

Lincoln Ojolo

Example of a covering letter disclosing a prison sentence

Karl Smith
Address
Telephone numbers
Email address

Chenab Mangat
Job title
Name of organisation
Address of organisation

Today's date

Application for position of Administrative Assistant

Dear Mr Mangat

Please find enclosed my application for the position of Administrative Assistant with XYZ Marketing.

I am eager to pursue a career in marketing and have recently completed the ABC distance certificate in marketing. I plan to continue my evening studies in marketing and have applied for a position on the DEF course. As you will see, I have several years' office experience and have experience using a range of software packages including Word and Excel. I have strong communication skills and solid organisational abilities, which were recently further enhanced through my experience of organising events for adults with learning difficulties.

I have, however, a conviction for theft which arose from financial hardship at the time and which no longer applies. I made a mistake and I have learned a tough and valuable lesson. I used my time in prison constructively by enrolling on the ABC Marketing Course in the hope that I could move my career in a positive direction after completing my sentence. I was also allowed out of prison on a day-release basis so that I could work as a volunteer in a day centre for adults with learning difficulties.

I have a good work track record and hope you will judge me on this rather than my past conviction, of which I am not proud. I am, of course, prepared to discuss this further at the interview.

Yours sincerely

Karl Smith

Richard Burroughs
Address
Telephone numbers
Email address

Mairead O'Gara
Job title
XYZ Public Relations
Address of organisation

Today's date

Application for position of Account Manager

Dear Mrs O'Gara

I read with interest your advertisement in the *Local Herald* of 6 June for the position of Account Manager, and have enclosed my CV as requested.

As you will see from my CV, I have several years' experience working on the PR accounts of many blue chip clients. I am methodical and organised in my approach to work and normally have a never-say-no attitude to client relationships. Unfortunately, such an approach was severely tested last year when I refused to take on the account of a tobacco firm. A committed anti-smoker, I felt I could not compromise my beliefs. Regretfully I got into an argument with my line manager about this and was summarily dismissed for insubordination. I am not proud of this argument and would like to make clear that this was out of character and something I never wish to repeat. My previous references are testimony to my ability and dedication.

I have a lot to offer XYZ Public Relations and would not let you down. I would welcome the opportunity to meet you to discuss this further.

Yours sincerely

Richard Burroughs

Emma Green
Address
Telephone numbers
Email address

Matthew Blue
Job title
ZZZ Sales
Address of organisation

Today's date

Application for position of graduate trainee: business strategy

Dear Mr Blue

I am writing in application for the graduate trainee scheme (specialising in business strategy, ref: 10625) as advertised on your website. Please find my CV attached as requested.

As you will see from my CV, I have an MBA from the University of Bath. I have a passionate interest in strategic business operations and would relish a career where I would be able to work with individual companies in an advisory role, monitoring and revising their business strategies. I initially felt that I should do this as an accountant. However, on reflection, I now know that my skills are best suited to the bigger picture (strategy), rather than the forensic detail of audited accounts (accountancy). During the probationary period of my last position, I came to the mutual conclusion with my employer that training to become an accountant was not the best use of my skills.

I would be happy to discuss this and how I could make a positive difference to your firm and your clients in more detail with you.

Yours sincerely

Emma Green

Example of a covering letter disclosing a disability

Sarah Granger
Address
Telephone numbers
Email address

Kwame Johnson
Job title
Name of organisation
Address of organisation

Today's date

Application for position of New Business Manager

Dear Mr Johnson

I read with interest your advertisement in the *Gazette* of November 16 for the position of New Business Manager, and have enclosed my CV as requested.

I thrive on the thrill of landing a new account and would relish the opportunities that your company presents for me to explore a new sector. In my previous role as New Business Co-ordinator, I introduced two new clients to the business that subsequently resulted in five contracts worth over £50,000 each.

I would welcome the opportunity to meet you to discuss how I could make a significant contribution. I do have a hearing impairment, however, and if you would like me to come for an interview there are a couple of things that could make the interview easier for both of us. If your building has a loop system, it would enhance my hearing ability, and I would be grateful if we could conduct the interview in a room where the system is active. I wear a digital hearing aid and normally have no problem in understanding colleagues and clients both in person and on the telephone. However, if your building has a noisy air conditioning system, it might also help if we could turn it down or off just for the duration of the interview.

Yours sincerely

Sarah Granger

Submitting a CV online

Many employers will ask you to apply online. This can involve completing an online application form or submitting your CV. Although the same rules apply to these as to paper-based CVs and applications, you will also need to consider further aspects such as the importance of key search terms and special techniques for completing online forms.

ONLINE CV AND APPLICATION KEY WORDS

CVs that are stored on an online database, as well as CVs and applications that are submitted for specific jobs online, are frequently not read in the first instance by a human. The whole reason a recruiter uses a computer for this stage is not to save you postage, it is so that the first round of selection and rejection of applications can be automated. The easiest way to do this is to program a search engine to find key words within the application or CV. No key words, no chance! It is vitally important, therefore, to think about what a search engine may be programmed to look for. The best way to do this is to carefully study the job requirements and boil your CV down to its barest ingredients.

Be key word savvy

The techniques you will need to employ on your CV or application are not so very different from those used by websites that try to get into the first few listings of a search engine's results pages (SERPs). In fact, SERPs placings are so keenly fought over that a whole industry called search engine optimisation (SEO) has grown up designed to aid websites in their attempt to get onto the first page of results from search engines such as Google, MSN, Ask or Yahoo. Thankfully, you will not have to try to second-guess which complex algorithm a search engine is employing this month. But you will still have to second-guess the words your recruiter deems important.

If you are responding to a job advertisement, this should be pretty straightforward. Look at the key requirements listed in the advertisement or person specification. Then make sure that these appear, word-for-word, in your CV. For example, if the advertisement calls for degree-level candidates with at least two years' experience in the retail industry. Your CV may show a 2:1 from

> ❝ You have to use key words in an application that will be vetted online, because the initial screening process is automated. ❞

Warwick and may say that you have worked for Tesco between 2004 and 2007. A person can deduce from this that you fit the basic requirements precisely, but programming a search engine to come to the same conclusion would be almost impossible. In this instance, and indeed with all CVs submitted online, your best approach is to provide an introductory paragraph marked 'Personal statement' that lists your skills. In the retail example this would begin, 'After graduating with a degree from Warwick University, gained three years' experience as a graduate trainee working in various departments of the grocery retailer, Tesco.' The key words here are: three years' experience; grocery retailer; degree; and University.

- Deconstruct the job advertisement or job specification so that it is nothing more than a list of skills and qualities.
- Make sure that every point on your deconstructed list is included on your CV in the clearest and most obvious way possible. Then you can be sure that the search engine will be able to give a 100 per cent positive match to all of the search criteria.

You can also trick the system by doing this even if you do not have a specific skill by still referring to it in your CV. For example, the job specification may assert that experience in PowerPoint would be beneficial. If you have no PowerPoint experience, instead of just leaving it off, you could write, 'Although I have no PowerPoint experience, I am fluent in a number of applications including Excel, Office and Adobe. I am confident that I could become proficient in PowerPoint quickly.' Particularly with the phrase 'proficient in PowerPoint', most search engines would find it hard to work out if you were a PowerPoint reject from this and would accept you. A human reading your application once it has been accepted by the search engine could consider your potential more thoughtfully and may decide that you are worth it despite your lack of PowerPoint skills.

Although it is harder to play around with language on an application form than on a CV, it is important to apply the same techniques to an application form. Online forms are 'read' in the same way as CVs according to key word searches, to give your application a chance, you still need to ensure those key words appear.

66 Turn the job specification into a list of requirements, and make sure your application meets them. 99

For more information on when application forms are used and how to fill them in, see pages 132–5.

What next?

Try to write your draft generic CV today. Once you have something on paper you will already be well on the way to preparing a winning CV.

1 Write a draft generic CV, listing your key skills.

2 Research the preferences of your industry and ask yourself:
   - Should I write in the first or third person?
   - How many pages is appropriate?
   - Should I opt for a conservative design or be more creative?
   - Should I email my CV?

3 Draw up a list of action and search engine appropriate key words.

4 Write a CV tailored directly to the needs of an individual job advertisement or person specification.

5 Tell the truth, but sell yourself.

6 Draft a covering letter, tailored to the requirements of the specific job. Use the letter as a platform from which you can sell yourself some more, or explain tricky issues in more detail.

7 Double-check it for errors.

So you have a perfect CV and covering letter, all you need now is the interview. But what do you do if your reply to the job advertisement is an application form? Can you just cut and paste your CV into their online form? Probably not. Read on to see why.

Application forms

Application forms are becoming an increasingly popular recruitment method, particularly among public sector employers who need to sort through a high volume of applications and need to be seen to be fair. All applicants are given the same questions, making it easier for the recruiter to make comparisons between candidates and providing a level playing field.

Types of application form

There are two main styles of application form; one takes a standard approach asking for personal details and why you are applying for the job, the other is a competence-based form asking you to give examples of your experience. All forms ask for basic details such as your name, address, contact details and education.

Standard application form

In addition to requesting basic information, the standard form tends to include a large box that asks why you are applying for the post and what skills and experience you bring. It is large because your potential employer wants you to elaborate on the details, giving solid examples of the skills you list. This is often the most important part of the form as it gives you the opportunity to set yourself apart from other candidates and really sell yourself.

Additional information: Occasionally, the information box is not included as part of the form, but is referred to as something called your 'supporting statement'. In these instances, you are expected to explain why you are perfect for the job on a separate piece of paper. If you are asked to do this, remember to put your name and the position you are applying for at the head of the paper.

Competence-based application form

In place of the single 'large box' or 'supporting statement', a competence-based application form asks you to give examples that demonstrate your competence in certain areas. It might ask you to describe a project or event for which you have been responsible, for example, or give details about a problem that you have solved. Opposite are some examples of competence-based questions for you to consider.

“ Give a range of specific, strong examples to show a broad spectrum of experience. ”

 An example of a filled-in standard application form is given on pages 122-7 and an example of a competence-based application form appears on pages 128-31.

- Can you give an example of where you think you have delivered excellent customer service?
- How would you motivate and encourage a member of your team?
- How do you ensure you meet your tasks/goals for the day?
- What do you consider to be your greatest personal achievement?
- What makes you a strong applicant for this position?

To answer these types of questions, consider the following pointers:

- Give specific, strong examples that are ideally quite recent.
- Choose a different example for each question; this will demonstrate that you have a broad spectrum of competence.
- If you cannot give any examples of what you have done in the workplace, think about what you have done outside work. Most recruiters are happy to accept examples that are taken from your home life, whether they are to do with a personal interest or hobby, or to do with your personal circumstances, such as household management, caring

Applications versus CVs

What are the key differences between application forms and CVs? Why do some employers prefer applications and some prefer CVs? Is there a case for requiring both?

The up-side of application forms
- **Ease of comparison:** Application forms enable recruiters to make direct comparisons between your skills and those of another applicant more quickly than CVs allow. The need for speed means that application forms tend to be used most often for sectors and roles where the number of applications submitted tends to be high, such as the public sector or management trainee roles. Some employers have a general form that they use for every recruit, regardless of the position they are hiring for.
- **Fairer treatment:** Many employers assert that the use of application forms is a much fairer way of going about the recruitment process; this way, you have to respond to the same questions and prompts as your competitors.

The down-side of application forms
- **An incomplete picture of your suitability for the job:** Recruiters claim that your ability to organise information is starkly illustrated through your CV. If your CV is confusing to read, messy or missing information, this can potentially say more about you than any answer on your application form.
- **They are bland:** Critics complain that application forms represent a bland version of CVs and take up far more paper as there needs to be space for both questions and answers.

Competence-based question: responding with a non-work answer

Give an example of a time when you have successfully risen to a challenge

As voluntary play leader of my son's toddler group, I conducted an audit of the group's toys, which resulted in several being thrown away due to damage, wear and tear. I wanted to replace these with new toys, but was reluctant to take too much away from the group's funds as we wanted to use this to pay for a planned outing to the zoo. I felt the answer was to raise money specifically for the toys and so organised a Teddy Bear's Picnic and Tea Party. The event was opened to all members of the toddler group, their elder siblings and neighbours of the community hall where we met. We sold refreshments at the event and held activities for the children that included icing (and eating!) your own biscuit for ten pence per go. As well as being great fun for the children, we raised £147 at the event and were able to buy more and bigger toys (including a new indoor slide) than we had initially hoped.

for your children or managing the financial affairs of a relative for example.

- If your recruiter wants you to stick to professional examples, the instructions on the application form should clearly state this.

The great thing about competence-based application forms is that they do much of the work for you and save any second-guessing. Remember, you must make clear that you have what a recruiter is looking for.

- If a question, or series of questions, asks you about how you like to prepare for a presentation, how you deal with misplaced telephone calls or how you deal with conflict, your recruiter wants to gauge your level of communication skills.
- If an application form contains more than one question that appears to ask about communication skills, you can be sure that it is an area that your recruiter is keenly interested in. So make sure in this instance that you stress your ability in this area by answering the questions with specific examples and, for a bit of extra punch, explaining in your covering letter that you consider good communication to be vital and including an extra example.

 When it comes to the interview stage, it is common to be asked for more details about the situations that you have described on your application form. So make sure that you are familiar with what you have written and can talk fluently about this, as well as other areas of your experience and skills.

Filling in an application form

Cut and paste information from your CV into an application form and you run the risk of failing to answer the question. This is an easy way for recruiters to weed out unsuitable applications at the first read through. Don't allow sloppiness to ruin your chances of getting that interview.

Some recruiters like to cover all bases and ask applicants to submit a CV in addition to completing an application form. On the whole, however, unless the job advertisement or application pack directs you otherwise, it is not a good idea to submit your CV along with the application form you have been asked to complete. Your CV will most likely just repeat much of the information included on the application form. Anything you would like to mention, but were unable to include on the form, can be put into your covering letter.

COMPLETING AN APPLICATION FORM

Before you start to complete an application form, it is a good idea to consider the following points.

- Copy the form BEFORE you start to fill it in. This will allow you to have a practice run, make mistakes and still have a clean form to copy your final answers on to.
- Always read the whole document before you start to fill it in, so that you can avoid an answer better suited to the next question.

- If the form is online and will not let you read the whole thing in advance, gather up as much information as you can and set aside sufficient time to work your way through it uninterrupted.
- If you are filling in the form by hand, always use a black or a dark blue pen.
- Concentrate hard on being neat; if necessary, write in capital letters.
- Follow all the instructions given. Failing to do so tells the recruiter you can't follow simple instructions.
- Answer every question or write 'not applicable' to show that you have read it and are not simply ignoring it.
- Check and double-check everything. Ask someone to check your first draft. Typos, spelling mistakes and grammar errors are as disastrous on your application form as they are on your CV.
- Stay organised. Keep a copy of your completed form and the covering letter you submit with it. If you are applying for more than one job, make sure you keep careful records of which application went to which employer.

❝ Copy the form before filling it in. ❞

115

The essentials of an effective supporting statement

The key to completing a good supporting statement is ensuring you tick all of your recruiter's boxes. The key to a brilliant one, however, is ticking those boxes in a coherent and organised way. You may be the best person for the job, but this will not come across if your text wanders about and the recruiter has to search for the answers. The worst thing you can do is submit a rambling story that attempts to explain why you have always wanted to do this job. One anecdote that reveals a eureka moment is fine. (Perhaps the moment when, as a child, you showed your father how to access the internet and you decided that you always wanted

❝ The best supporting statements tick all the recruiter's boxes. ❞

Example requests for supporting statements

- Please supply additional information that you feel appropriate to your application, including achievements and skills gained, which you consider relevant to the post and that relate to the criteria contained in the person specification. Continue on separate sheets if necessary. Please number any additional sheets.
- Why did you choose us as a potential employer? What relevant skills do you feel you have to offer?
- Use this section to outline the skills and experience you have gained in paid, unpaid or voluntary work, work at home, or through your studies or leisure activities, which you think are relevant to the job for which you are applying. Please indicate the extent to which you believe your skills, abilities and experience meet the job requirements (as outlined in the advertisement and any additional information provided).
- Please use this space to add further comments in support of your application and to explain why you are applying to The XYZ Group of Companies plc. (Continue on a separate sheet if necessary.)
- Supporting statement maximum 1,000 words. Please show how you are able to meet the specific requirements of the person specification for this post.

 For more examples of well-written supporting statements, see the sample CVs given in the previous chapter on pages 80, 83, 88, 90, 94 and 98.

Jargon buster

Personal statement A term that can be interchangeably used to refer to the short personal profile normally found on a CV, or the longer supporting statement that is common to many standard application forms

to know more than everyone else about computers and became an expert in your field of programming.) But if you submit such a story without also listing why you are the person for the job, your application will fail.

- **Identify what boxes need ticking.** The easiest way to do this is to comb the person specification for them. Nearly all applications that require such additional information will include a person specification as part of the application pack. (Application packs often include information about the organisation too.) If you don't have one, check with your prospective employer; perhaps you should have been sent one and it was missed out of your pack. If that wasn't the case, your recruiter may offer you an impromptu description there and then, so make sure you have a pen and paper to hand when you call. And if that still doesn't yield results, check the job advertisement carefully, as the requirements for the job are normally listed within it too.

- Take each requirement from the person specification or job advertisement and make a list in the same order that they appear. Then, when you apply your own qualities to those asked for, make sure they appear in the same order again. This will help your recruiter tick your boxes in record time as they won't have to search through your statement, and it will help earn you plenty of points.
- **Take each requirement in turn,** identify it as a skill or quality you possess and then – and this is the crucial part – provide an example. Remember not to do this in a vacuum. You should also demonstrate your understanding of why that skill or quality is important.

For example in Alice's case study (see overleaf), the job description for an account manager working in the design services department of a county council lists as its first requirement: 'To provide advice, consultancy and support to managers and staff at all levels (and other organisations where appropriate) on anything of a visual nature that has an impact on the County Council's brand and that requires professional design input.' The first paragraphs of her supporting statement specifically address this.

❝Show you meet each requirement in the same order as they were listed in the brief.❞

117

Case Study | Alice

When Alice wrote her supporting statement, she specifically addressed the job description's first requirement:

I believe that communication is at the heart of design services and my ability to communicate well on many different levels, including in the creative process, is my strongest quality.

In my current position as account handler for XYZ Design, I do not simply manage accounts but am proactive in all stages of the creative process. This includes taking part in team-wide brainstorming sessions at the visual ideas stage, as well as providing advice on practical issues, such as the availability of individual printing houses.

I am responsible for liaising between clients, designers, managers and outsourced providers. One recent example was a poster campaign for the council's Housing Department. I took a verbal brief from the Head of Housing, wrote it up and checked this with the client before presenting it in partnership with my account manager in a briefing meeting for the design team.

In the following ideas session, two of my suggestions were developed into a working draft of five ideas that I presented to the Housing Department along with the creative director. One of my ideas was chosen as the design route. I commissioned the photographer, copywriter and printer and ensured that each was fully briefed and given the appropriate purchase order. The project was completed on time and the Housing Department has reported positive feedback on the campaign.

Further essentials for an effective supporting statement include:

- Structure the statement into sections. It will make it a more attractive proposition for the reader. All of us, even the most hardened human resources professional recruiter, can lean towards being lazy readers. Being presented with several small chunks to read rather than one long tract will always appear more enticing. Divide the statement with subheadings, which should relate directly to the requirement listed in the person specification or job advertisement. The subhead in Alice's case study, therefore, would read: 'Providing advice, consultancy and support'.
- If you have been provided with a word limit, stick to it.
- If you are invited to use additional sheets, expand onto just one more piece of paper. Remember to put your name, the title of the job you are applying for and the job reference number at the head of any supplementary pages.

ANSWERING TRICKY QUESTIONS

These are examples of tougher questions that you may find on an application form and the best way in which you should approach answering them.

Q What are your reasons for leaving your previous employment?

Although you should never include reasons for leaving your last employment on your CV, this is a question that is commonly included on all types of application form. The best way to approach it is to be positive. There may be several reasons why you are looking for a new job. Where possible, leave out the negative reasons and include the positive. If you want to leave your current position because you don't want to work with a particular colleague, try to avoid saying this and find alternative reasons instead. For example, you could say that you have gone as far as you could go in your current position and are eager to explore new challenges. If you are applying for a job that is at a higher level than the one you are on, you could say that there were no opportunities for promotion with your current company.

If you have been dismissed from a previous job, it is almost impossible to fudge this question. As explained on page 179, lying isn't an option. If you are found out (and one call to your last employer would reveal all), you could be dismissed for dishonesty. The best way to present yourself is to explain what happened and why it will never happen again. There probably will not be enough room to do this on the application form, in which case you should write 'see accompanying letter', or 'see supporting statement'.

Example letters showing how you might disclose the fact that you have been dismissed are included in the section on covering letters in Chapter 4 on pages 101–7.

Q Have you ever been convicted of a criminal offence?

This is another example of information that you should ideally try to leave off your CV but that is often directly asked in an application form. Remember that minor offences such as speeding and other driving offences that incur points on your licence are also convictions that may need to be declared. See also 'dealing with disclosure' on page 102.

If you are applying for a job and you have a conviction that is not yet spent and there is room on your application to explain your conviction, do so. If not, put 'see accompanying letter'. If your conviction is old, support your case by pointing this out, especially if, for example you were convicted as a teenager and

Tricky questions needn't be limited to the application forms. If you get to the interview stage, you might have to face more. See pages 178–91 for examples of different types of questions.

have now matured and settled down, perhaps with a mortgage and a family of your own. If it sounds more serious than it is, you should also say so. If serving a prison sentence has left a gap in your employment history, you can also write 'not available for work, see covering letter' on your application.

❝ If your answer isn't going to look good, try to give an explanation. ❞

Q Are you taking any form of medication?

Despite the introduction of the Disability Discrimination Act, a surprising number of application forms ask quite detailed questions about your health history. This may include questions such as:

- How many days absent from work have you taken in the last 12 months?
- Are you currently in good health? If you answer no, please give brief details.
- Are you a smoker or non-smoker?
- Do you have any recurring illnesses?
- Do you consider yourself fit and able to carry out the duties and responsibilities of the post for which you have applied?
- Are you taking any form of medication?

You will need to approach such questions with care. Declaring 'no' to the question that asks if you are fit and able to carry

out the duties and responsibilities of the post, however, will probably mean instant rejection. Saying you took three days off work for ill health last year when you really took 20 is a lie. It is a fact that can be easily checked with your last employer and, if you are caught out in the lie, you either won't be offered the job in the first place or may be sacked if you have been given it.

If you need to give an answer that doesn't look good, try where possible to give an explanation. As with the examples above, if there is room, explain yourself on the form and if there is not enough space on the form, write 'see covering letter' and explain yourself there.

- If you are a smoker but have decided to quit, say so.
- If you have a recurring illness or have had a lot of days off sick, concentrate on what kind of impact your health will have on your future performance.
- If you are getting better or have begun a new medication, you can say this. For example, perhaps you suffer from a chronic illness such as arthritis. If, last year, you had a series of flare-ups but have now settled into a new medication that seems to reduce the incidents of flare-ups, you can explain this in your covering letter.

Your recruiter will be looking for reassurance that you will be able to do the job and won't cost the company too much money in time off. Where possible, offer as much reassurance as you can.

Remember your rights. It is illegal under the Disability Discrimination Act to discriminate against you because of illness, which can be considered a disability. This includes any diagnosis of cancer whether terminal or not, a mental health condition, or a condition such as dyslexia. In addition to making reasonable changes to your workplace, the recruiting company is also legally required to make adjustments for the recruitment process if requested by you.

ETHNIC ORIGINS

Many employers include a section on ethnic origins. They are legally not allowed to use this information to discriminate against you and many employers keep this information away from the recruitment process so that it does not even have the chance to affect recruitment decisions on an unconscious basis.

Employers ask for such information to monitor the diversity of the applications they receive. This is then used by employers to help develop appropriate policies and procedures regarding diversity and equal opportunities. For example, if it was revealed that only British white males applied for vacancies within an organisation, that organisation could then look into its procedures to see if there was a reason for this. Perhaps the vacancy was advertised in a place that was not normally accessed by women or by people of different nationalities or ethnic origins. If this was found to be the case, the organisation might be able to make changes to the way it advertises its vacancies.

If you feel that you have been discriminated against because of your age, ethnicity, gender or disability, contact the Commission for Equality and Human Rights (see box, below) or your local Citizens Advice Bureau (www.adviceguide.org.uk) for further advice.

Commission for Equality and Human Rights

The Commission for Equality and Human Rights (CEHR) is a non-departmental public body that was launched in October 2007 with a remit to reduce inequality, eliminate discrimination and strengthen good relations between people and protect human rights.

It brings together the work of three former Commissions; the Commission for Racial Equality, the Disability Rights Commission and the Equal Opportunities Commission. To contact the CEHR, see www.equalityhumanrights.com or call 0800 0181 259.

Application form – AN Other Council

Please complete all sections in full

Position applied for Senior support officer

Post reference number 0123

Closing date 01/01/08

How did you hear about the vacancy? Local newspaper job advertisement

PERSONAL DETAILS

Surname Mohammed

First name(s) Sulaiman

Title (Mr/Mrs/Miss/Ms/other) Mr

UK National Insurance Number 123456789

UK/EC Passport holder YES/~~NO~~

Telephone numbers

Daytime 01234 5678910

Evening 01234 5678910

Mobile 07777 012345

Email address Suliaman.Mohammed@emailaddress.com

Full postal address, including postcode and country 17 Church Lane, Anytown, AT1 1AT, UK

Are you related to any councillor or employee of this council? No

If yes, please state who N/A

Do you require a work permit? No

DISABILITY

Please tell us about any disability, as defined under the terms of the Disability Act 1995, which may or may not affect your ability to do the job

I use a wheelchair

If you would like any assistance if you are called for interview, please provide details

I need to use a lift or a ramp in place of stairs, but other than that I need no assistance

Position applied for Senior support officer   **Reference number** 0123   **Closing date** 01/01/08

HISTORY OF ANY CONVICTIONS

Have you ever been convicted of an offence within the terms of the Rehabilitation of Offenders Act 1974? If yes, please give details

No

HEALTH HISTORY

State number of days and number of separate instances you were absent through sickness in the last 12 months

Three days on a single occasion

EMPLOYMENT HISTORY

Name and address of employer Anycounty County Council

Job title Manager

Salary £25,000

Date commenced 02 August 2004

Leaving date 02 February 2008

Reasons for leaving Career progression

Duties and responsibilities Supervise work of office staff, conducting recruitment, inductions and appraisals.

Oversee payroll and timesheets.

Review performance with senior management.

Manage office budget and order stationery, office equipment and furniture.

Organise office maintenance and repair.

Name and address of employer Anycounty Borough Council

Job title Office manager

Salary £21,000

Date commenced 12 June 2001

Leaving date 01 August 2004

Reasons for leaving Career progression

EMPLOYMENT HISTORY cont.

Duties and responsibilities Supervise work of office staff, manage payroll and timesheets.

Manage office budget, including petty cash.

Order stationery, office equipment and furniture.

Organise office maintenance and repair.

Arrange travel, meetings and appointments.

Name and address of employer Anycounty Borough Council

Job title Office assistant

Salary £16,000

Date commenced 17 September 2000

Leaving date 11 June 2001

Reasons for leaving Promotion

Duties and responsibilities Manage incoming telephone calls, emails and faxes.

Keep appointments diary and arrange all travel and accommodation.

Take minutes of meetings.

Deputise for the manager in her absence.

Manage files and information storage.

EDUCATION & TRAINING

Date	Establishment	Subject	Level and Grade
1991–1996	De Montfort School	8 GCSEs incl. English, Maths and Science	A–C
1996–1998	Stanley Jones Sixth Form College	English, biology, geography	C, C, D
1998–2000	London South Bank University	Business Studies	HND
January 2002	Chartered Institute of Purchasing & Supply	eProcurement and process integration	In-company training

Position applied for Senior support officer **Reference number** 0123 **Closing date** 01/01/08

MEMBERSHIP OF PROFESSIONAL BODIES

Name of association	Grade of membership	Date achieved	Exam yes/no
N/A			

Do you have a current driving licence?
YES/~~NO~~   If yes, indicate as appropriate: Car   ~~HGV~~   ~~Motorcycle~~
Please give details of any endorsements
Do you have access to transport for work purposes? YES/~~NO~~

ADDITIONAL INFORMATION
Please supply additional information that you feel appropriate to your application, including achievements and skills gained, which you consider relevant to the post and that relate to the criteria contained in the person specification. Continue on separate sheets if necessary. Please number any additional sheets.

Administrative support

I relish providing administrative support because I recognise that a team can only succeed in meeting its targets if this support is excellent and ongoing, and I enjoy playing my part in a winning team. In my current position as office manager for Anycounty County Council, I introduced new project management software to my department, which enabled me to keep central control over all of the department's resources. In addition to researching and procuring the software, I also trained seven clerical staff in its use. Since its introduction, the Department Director has reported an improvement in the whole department's productivity and I was invited to play a central part in rolling out my system to the Council's remaining key departments.

Planning

In each of my previous roles as office assistant and office manager in Council departments, one of my key responsibilities has been in planning. From co-ordinating diaries and arranging meetings to running the office budget, planning has been central in all of my work. In addition, I also see forward planning as an integral part of my procurement duties and I have ensured that for all of the past four years that I have worked in my current job, my office has never run out of stock.

ADDITIONAL INFORMATION cont.
Communication skills

In recognition of my good communication and negotiation skills, I was invited to become an informal conflict resolution manager in my previous position as office manager in Anytown Borough Council. If there ever was an example of conflict between staff (both between and within departments), I would work with a senior member of HR to find an amicable resolution. This usually meant an informal chat with each person in turn before bringing them together in a more structured meeting. I was responsible for conducting the informal chat, while my HR colleague ran the structured meeting. We found this was an excellent and low-key way of achieving mutually agreed resolutions to a range of disagreements.

IT literacy

I have completed every level of IT training, both voluntary and compulsory, available at Anycounty County Council. I am fluent in all of the MS Office suite of programs including, in particular, Word, Excel, PowerPoint and Project. One of my current duties is to translate notes from my departmental colleagues into PowerPoint presentations. These are used in presentations made both within and outside the Council.

Responsibility

I am the nominated First Aider of the department. Because more volunteers than were needed came forward for the position, the department held a secret ballot to decide who the nominated First Aider should be. I won the ballot. It is a responsibility I take very seriously and I attend a First Aid course to update my skills every six months.

Position applied for <u>Senior support officer</u> Reference number <u>0123</u> Closing date <u>01/01/08</u>

EQUALITIES MONITORING

To help us check our recruitment procedures are in accordance with Council policy and legislative requirements, the Council monitors the ethnic makeup of its employees and those applying for employment. In order to help monitor the effectiveness of its policy, and for no other reason, please complete the following section. This information will be treated as confidential and kept separately from your application. It will not be available to those interviewing.

Gender: Male ~~Female~~

White: British _____   Irish _____   Other _____

Mixed: White/Black Caribbean _____   White/Black African _____

White/Asian <u>Yes</u>   Other mixed background _____

Asian or Asian British:

Indian _____   Pakistani _____

Bangladeshi _____   Other Asian background _____

Black or British:

Caribbean _____   African _____   Other Black background _____

Other ethnic groups:

Chinese _____   Any other ethnic group _____

REFEREES

Please give the details of two people, not relatives, who have consented to act as referees on your behalf, one of whom must be your present or most recent employer. Confidential references will be taken up, normally by letter, before interview unless you place a X next to the name to indicate that <u>you do not wish your referee to be approached</u>. No appointment will be confirmed until satisfactory references have been received.

Ibrahim Vohra	Sally Kingston
Departmental Head of Procurement	Head of HR
Anycounty County Council	Anytown Borough Council
Address	Address
Telephone number	Telephone number
Email address	Email address

Example of a (completed) competence-based application form

Catering Company Application Form

All sections, including the Equal Opportunities Monitoring form, should be completed by all applicants, except where otherwise indicated. Please note that the information that you have given in this form, such as your name and address, will be held on Catering Company recruitment records. It will not be disclosed outside Catering Company without your consent.

Job Title   Marketing assistant

Form to be returned by: 05.05.08

Where did you see this vacancy advertised?   Catering Company website

Surname   Wilkinson

First name(s)   Lucinda   **Mr/Mrs/Miss, or preferred title**   Ms

Preferred contact address
Dean's School Hall of Residence
The University of Manchester
Oxford Road
Manchester
M13 9PL

Telephone (home)   01234 567890   **Telephone (work)**   N/A

Mobile   07712 345678   **E-mail** Lucinda@emailaddress.co.uk

Return completed form to: Uzma Ghuman

Internal applicants only
It is essential that this section is completed in order for your application to be progressed.

Please write your staff number here –

My current contract is – Continuing ☐   **Fixed-term** ☐ N/A

Job Title Marketing assistant   **Name** Lucinda Wilkinson

QUALIFICATIONS & TRAINING

Starting with the most recent, please give details of your education/training.
Include details of your school, college or organisation; qualifications or course name, and grades obtained.

2004–2007	University of Kent	BA (Hons) Psychology and Sociology 2:1 (Courses included Interpersonal behaviour, group behaviour, business enterprises)
2002–2004	Summerfield School, Dorset	A levels in History (B), Sociology (B) and French (C)
1997–2002	Summerfield School, Dorset	9 GCSEs at grade C or above including English Language (A) and Mathematics (A)

EMPLOYMENT HISTORY

Starting with your present or most recent job, please give a summary of all employment, including any freelance and relevant unpaid work.
Include name of employer, nature of business, job title and brief description of your responsibilities. Please include salary and benefits (internal candidates also give grade).

June 2006–August 2006   ABC Marketing   Summer internship where I assisted with summer campaign for XYZ client to launch new fizzy drink flavour. I was responsible for briefing copywriter on leaflet language and for assisting in the co-ordination of the PR launch.

June 2005–Sept 2005   US Summer Camp   Camp counsellor for children aged 8–13. Organised social, sporting and art activities. Trained in First Aid.

Sept 2004–January 2005 The Smugglers   Part-time waitress for city centre restaurant popular with tourists. Balanced part-time work with study, worked as part of a team, and thrived under pressure during busy periods.

Job Title Marketing assistant   **Name** Lucinda Wilkinson

SKILLS, ABILITIES & EXPERIENCE

Use this section to outline the skills and experience you have gained in paid, unpaid or voluntary work, work at home, or through your studies or leisure activities, which you think are relevant to the job for which you are applying. Please indicate the extent to which you believe your skills, abilities and experience meet the job requirements (as outlined in the advertisement and any additional information provided).

Describe a situation where you demonstrated strong communication skills

My communication skills will provide a vital asset to my marketing team, both in my ability to persuade others and my willingness to work in a team. As a camp counsellor, it was one of my responsibilities to ensure my group of children kept their own living quarters clean and tidy. Some children were reluctant to do this. In order to motivate all of the group, I liaised with the other counsellors and devised an inter-group competition, where each group competed against each other for the tidiest quarters. A prize was given to the group with the most points each Friday. The children loved the competition and the counsellors enjoyed taking turns to procure the best prize every week.

Are you able to work effectively in a team?

My team-working abilities are best illustrated through my membership of the University basketball team. Although by far the shortest member of the starting five, as 'point-guard' I regulate the tempo of the game in conjunction with instruction from the team's captain.

Would you describe yourself as someone with drive, or someone who prefers to be driven?

I have drive. Once I start a project, I never give in. Last year I was part of a group of friends that applied for the London Marathon ballot. Only one of our group was successful in the ballot. Undeterred, I applied for and succeeded in getting a golden bond place for Cancer Research UK. Having never been a runner before, I spent six months focusing on a regime of structured training. I completed the course in four hours and 47 minutes and raised £1,326.00 for Cancer Research.

Job Title Marketing assistant   **Name** Lucinda Wilkinson

Catering Company is committed to making selection and interview processes fair for all applicants. If you have any access requirements such as enabling equipment or if you require a support worker, please provide more detail below: N/A

EXTERNAL APPLICANTS ONLY

Please give the name and address of two referees. These should be your most recent employers, including your present employer where applicable, or a relevant academic principal. Personal referees should be given only when there is no previous employer or educational establishment to which reference can be made.

1. Name
    Job title
    Address
    Postcode
    Telephone
    E-mail
    Relationship

2. Name
    Job title
    Address
    Postcode
    Telephone
    E-mail
    Relationship

I agree that any offer of employment with Catering Company is subject to satisfactory references, medical information supplied and a medical examination (if required).

Can references be taken up without further permission from you?

Your first referee Yes   **Your second referee** Yes

SIGNATURE

I confirm that the information supplied by me on this form is correct.

Signature signed   **Date** dated

You will be asked to demonstrate eligibility to work in the UK during the selection process.

Online application forms

There are two main styles of online application forms: those you can download (or at least print off in advance) and those you cannot. Within these, just like paper applications, you will find standard and competence-based forms. In addition, you may come across interactive application forms that alter their questions as you type in your answers.

INTERACTIVE TECHNOLOGY

On its most basic level, a form may not allow you to proceed to the next page until you have completed the information on the page you are on. The registration pages for a large number of employers' sites are like this, from EasyJet to Bloomberg. If you are applying to an international employer, one of the first questions they may ask is what country you want to work in. The questions you are given after you have answered this one would therefore be made applicable to the requirements of the job in the country that you have stated.

Such a geographical question would also have implications for recruiting techniques due to employment laws that may differ in each jurisdiction. For example, in the UK, with your permission, employers may keep your details on a database of unsuccessful candidates for future contact if you appear suitable for an upcoming position in the company. The same may not be true in other countries. France and Germany, for example, have data-protection policies that tend to be stricter than those in the UK or the Netherlands.

**Technology is now so advanced that an application form can be tailored to ask you questions applicable to, say, the country you want to work in.**

 Some online application forms are timed. The Civil Service Fast Stream form is like this. You are given a fixed number of days to complete each stage of the application and each of the online tests is subject to a time limit.

APPLICATION FORMS YOU CAN READ IN ADVANCE

Some employers will allow you to download, or at least read and print off, an application form in its entirety. These are closest to paper forms (often an uploaded version of a paper form) and the easiest type to complete. This is because you can see all the questions before you start to complete the form and, therefore, prepare for it. Applications submitted online often don't allow you to expand on supplementary sheets in the way that paper ones do, so your answers need to be as succinct and direct as possible.

> **"** Make your answers as succinct as possible on online applications because you don't always have supplementary sheets to expand on. **"**

Completing an application form you can read in advance

- Print off the form and complete it by hand first. This will allow you to correct mistakes before you transcribe your perfect answers direct to the online version.

- Check and then double-check all spellings, grammar and your tick-list of key words.

- If you have a tricky area to disclose, possibly a prison sentence or a dismissal, instead of directing the recruiter to your covering letter (as you probably won't have one), leave the tricky question unanswered and put, 'Please contact for further details'. In that way you can, at least, defend yourself in an email, letter or phone call as appropriate.

- Approach both competence-based and standard questions in exactly the same way as you would a paper application form.

 Paper applications were covered earlier in this chapter. If you have turned straight to these pages because you have an online application form to fill in, it would be as well to read the text on pages 112–31 to get as much advice as possible.

APPLICATION FORMS YOU CANNOT READ IN ADVANCE

Some online application forms will only allow you to proceed to the next page of questions once you have completed and submitted the first page. Approach this style of application form with care. The last thing you need is to regret typing in an answer and be unable to go back and alter it. Some recruiters also use **applicant–tracking systems** to monitor the progress of any given applicant through their recruitment process. An applicant who completes a form in one, smooth sitting may appear more able than one who has three or four interrupted attempts, possibly over a number of days.

Use the tips given opposite to help complete an online application. They may make the process sound daunting, but don't be put off. Some forms are longer than others and some are more demanding than others. And in recognition that they need to attract applicants as much as an applicant wants to appear attractive, the current trend among employers is to keep online applications to an exercise that doesn't take more than half an hour. Whether this includes preparation time, however, is unlikely.

❝ Take extreme care submitting information on online forms that are submitted page by page, but try not to be too slow, as your rate of progress may be tracked. **❞**

Jargon buster

Applicant-tracking system Online tool designed to help a recruiter monitor the progress of any given applicant through their recruitment process
Thread Topic of conversation addressed by group of forum or chatroom users

 The Civil Service uses online applications for its Fast Stream programme. See its website, www.faststream.gov.uk, for further advice on how to access and complete its application process. Much of this is also applicable to other employers.

Completing an application form you cannot read in advance

- Do some homework before you start. Scour blogs and forums, starting a new **thread** if necessary, to find out from previous applicants what sort of questions the form asks. Act on that knowledge.
- If the form includes any competency tests, perhaps mathematical reasoning for an accountancy position for example, practise a few before you sit down to the form. Make sure you also have scrap paper, a pencil and a calculator to hand.
- If the form includes psychometric tests, practise a few questions first so that you can feel confident when the time comes to answer some for real. (For more information on these tests, read up on recruitment testing in Chapter 7.)
- Read everything you can about the company before you start. Read the organisation's own website, as well as anything you can find in an online search or archived in newspaper sites. If the form then asks questions that require a prior knowledge of the company, it should at least ring a bell with you, so that if you can't remember the answer exactly, you should know where to find it quickly.
- Gather everything you could possibly need to fill in the form. This includes your CV or a prompt sheet that includes your education dates, grades and your work history and tick list of key words.
- If you think they may want references, find your referees' contact details before you log-on.

- If you think they may want your passport number (it is possible that a cabin crew or pilot position would ask for this), fetch it before you begin.
- Write out possible answers to common competency-based questions and standard questions shown earlier in the chapter (see pages 112–14). If your online form presents you with a similar question, you can copy or adapt your ready-made (and, therefore, hopefully more eloquent) answer.
- Ensure that you double-check every page for silly typos before you click onto the next page.
- If you can, print off the pages as you complete them so that you have a record of your application. If the program will not let you do this, jot down notes on a piece of paper.
- You won't need to copy down every GCSE grade again, but it is a good idea to note your answers to more general questions, so that you can refresh yourself on what you actually said prior to your interview.
- Taking care may also help you if the internet connection is lost and you find that you have to start your application again from scratch.
- Shut yourself away and focus on the form. If you are at home, ignore all distractions. If you are in an internet café, book for a longer period than you think you will need. (If you have time left over, you can always join a chatroom for a while.)

What next?

Put what you have learnt into practice and make your application sparkle.

1 Carefully consider the points for completing an application form and practise everything you can before you fill in anything.

2 Check on the special online tips listed in Chapter 5 before you tackle an online application form.

3 Answer every question and don't lie.

4 Get creative. Think of interesting anecdotes to illustrate your experience and set your application apart from everyone else's.

5 Double-check the form before you seal the envelope or press send.

You may have sent off an application to every job advertisement you can find, but what about the ones that have only been revealed to a recruitment agency? For more details on how recruitment agencies can enhance your job search, see Chapter 6.

Recruitment agencies

UK recruitment is big business. In 2007, the industry turned over in excess of £24.8 billion and its current growth (up from just £3.5 billion in 1992) is showing no signs of slowing. Recruitment agencies place more than 700,000 employees in permanent work every year and another 1.4 million people in temporary positions. In addition to this, the industry directly employs over 97,000 people.

6

What does an agency do?

If there is a job for something, you can pretty much guarantee there is a recruitment agency or headhunter specialising in it somewhere. But what do they actually do and, most importantly, will they enhance your chances of finding the right job?

Recruitment consultants are a little like estate agents in so far as their remit requires them to introduce buyers to suitable sellers and vice versa. In this case you are the 'buyer' and the 'seller' is your potential employer. The recruitment agency is normally paid by the employer, either through a set fee or through commission paid on the successful placing of candidates. Some agencies will also become your 'employer' or labour provider, taking on the payroll burden of organising your wages and deducting your tax and national insurance at source. In these situations, the agency will charge the employer a handling fee.

The pros and cons of finding work through a recruitment agency

Pros

- You can spread your net wider and increase your chances of finding a job by looking for work in a different location.
- You can leave the hard work to someone else. Recruitment agents spend a lot of effort trawling job boards and often use specialist software tools to help them in their search for new vacancies.
- You can get tailored advice from someone who understands your objectives.
- If you live overseas and want to work in the UK, some agencies will help organise accommodation for you. This is most common in sectors recruiting for unskilled jobs, such as agriculture and food processing.

Cons

- You may earn more if you are employed directly. The recruitment agency charges your employer a fee for its service. To cover his or her costs, the employer may try to pay you less to cover the fee.
- If you sign up with several recruitment agencies, you run the risk of being presented for the same job several times (once by each agency). This is more likely to annoy or even confuse the recruiter than enhance your chances of success.
- Recruitment agencies will not put you forward for a job if there is no chance that they will get paid for the transaction, so unless you search for jobs yourself, you could miss out on your perfect job.

The service you receive from a recruitment consultancy can vary hugely and is largely dependent on factors such as size, location and area of speciality. If an agency has a local office, you can visit them in person and perhaps complete some tests to help assess your suitability for various roles. If an agency does not have an office near to you, you may complete all of your dealings with the consultants online and via the telephone. Many agency websites also act as job boards and list available vacancies. Some agencies exist exclusively online.

ESTABLISHING WHAT YOU WANT TO DO AND WHY

Agencies might do this through an informal discussion, or they might ask you to fill out an assessment form. Most agencies get paid when they place a candidate, so it makes good business sense for them to encourage you to explore a wide range of careers. If you are not entirely sure what you want to do, this can be really useful as the agency can help you to investigate your options. If you are sure that you only

want to work in marketing and your agent keeps steering you towards sales jobs, however, this could be deeply frustrating. To avoid this, be as clear as you can about what you want. If the agent still does not listen to you, go to another recruitment agency. It is a competitive marketplace out there and another agency is bound to want to snap you up.

YOUR CV

Your consultancy will also ask you to provide them with your CV. Depending on their level of service, they may work on this with you and help you create the style of CV they believe employers will look for. They can charge for this service but not for registering you with them.

WHAT YOU CAN EXPECT

What you can expect from your recruitment agency will vary between each one and on the type of job you want to go for. For example, you might receive a typing test if you want to apply for a position in office administration. (See also the box, below.)

The basics from a recruitment agency

- Job vacancy email or text alerts
- Online job boards
- CV workshops
- Practice interviews
- Practice recruitment tests
- Skills tests, such as typing and numeracy
- Salary negotiation (on your behalf)

What to ask your recruitment agency

The Recruitment and Employment Confederation (REC) is the trade body that supports and represents the recruitment industry. Members of REC comply with codes aimed at giving you a high standard of service and they are subject to REC complaints and disciplinary procedures. If you plan to look for work through a recruitment agency, REC recommends the following tips:

- Always ask the recruitment consultancy for a copy of the CV they are intending to send to clients on your behalf.
- Ask the recruitment consultancy to explain its policy on submitting your CV or details to a prospective employer.
- Avoid missing opportunities by making sure you stay in close contact with the consultancy and bear in mind that employers often put consultancies under a great deal of time pressure.

> **!** **Don't leave all of the responsibility of finding work to the agency. You should check the agency's website regularly in case there are jobs listed that are of interest to you but slightly outside your profile and therefore not on your agency's radar.**

- Tell your agency if you are happy not to be consulted on each occasion they put you forward for a job, but inform them in writing of any companies that you do not wish to receive your CV.
- Only allow the consultancy that first contacts you about a specific vacancy to act on your behalf.
- Always ask the recruitment consultancy if it is an REC member.

Before your recruiter starts work it is vital that you create a few ground rules. For example, if an agency plans to send your CV to an employer on your behalf, consider whether you would want them to write your covering letter for you. Remember, you are entitled to see correspondence sent on your behalf. Don't forget that recruitment agencies are run by humans too. They can make mistakes and may produce a CV that may not represent you as professionally as you would like. Ensure your agency fully briefs you on the role they want to submit your application for before they send off your CV. Recruitment agencies also have a legal obligation to check on your working status; they must ask whether you have the right to work in the UK.

A single recruitment agency will have many clients, so make time to call them on a regular basis so they do not forget about you and, above all, update them on your career achievements or experience.

 To access the Recruitment and Employment Confederation directory of employment agencies, see www.rec.uk.com.

SPECIALIST AGENCIES

Agencies range from nationwide generalists, such as Manpower, and regional generalists, such as Persona in the South East, to nationwide and regional specialists who tend to focus on one or a small group of industry sectors or candidate types. For example, Rockall Recruitment focuses on the construction industry in Wales and ITN Mark Education specialises in recruiting teachers, supply staff, nursery nurses and classroom assistants for schools across the UK and internationally.

The Graduate Recruitment Bureau finds permanent positions for graduates in the UK, and Chase International is an international recruitment agency that specialises in the recruitment of senior executives. Bluefire Consulting is fairly representative of an agency that covers more than one specialism. It focuses on a range of areas, from IT and Telecoms to Commercial and Finance.

Some agencies focus solely on temporary positions, some on permanent and the majority, such as office and secretarial staffing consultant Office Angels, on both. These are simply a small example of the range of recruitment agencies that currently operate in the UK.

Many university careers offices carry lists of agencies and their specialisms. Alternatively, enter your sector or hoped-for job title along with the word 'recruitment' into an online search engine in order to find a selection of agencies that may be able to represent you.

If an agency specialises in a particular sector, you could talk to their experts about the state of the industry. An expert in telecoms should know, for example, if the sector is buoyant and recruitment is high. They may also be able to tell you about 'hotspots', areas of the country that feature clusters of businesses from a particular sector. Bristol, for example, has many creative industries. If you wanted to work in a creative agency, moving to Bristol may help advance your career.

Make checks

Check out the work a recruitment agency does before you ask them to put you on their books. For example, there may be little point in approaching a specialist in the construction industry if you wanted to get into catering.

The easiest way to do this is to look on their website. A quick phone call to the agency in question may also answer your queries, although they may want to sign you up regardless of their focus. Think carefully before you agree to this, the last thing you need is to find yourself attending interviews for jobs you don't really want, or being presented in a way that you suspect could have been done better elsewhere.

 Website addresses for each of the agencies mentioned above are given in Useful Addresses on page 214.

LOOKING OVERSEAS

Under the rules of the European Economic Area (**EEA**), if you are a European citizen, you are free to live and work in any of the 25 EEA member states, as well as Norway, Lichtenstein and Iceland. This massively expands your opportunities for employment. One of the best ways to start exploring these opportunities is to sign up with an agency that specialises in finding work in a particular country or focuses on an industry in a number of different countries. Twinserve (www.twinserve.com), for example, specialises in international recruitment for the electronics industry. It has offices in the UK and the Netherlands, as well as partners in Germany and France.

There are several advantages to using a recruitment agency when you want to find work overseas. In addition to helping you to find a job, specialist agencies should be able to advise you on requirements such as visas or permits and help you with local rules and employment legislation.

Applying for jobs in the UK from overseas

Some agencies specialise in finding jobs for people coming to the UK from overseas. If you are not exempt from the need for a work permit, but have degree-level qualifications or specialist skills, you may be able to take advantage of the Highly Skilled Migrant Programme (HSMP). Entry to the programme depends on a points system. You are awarded points in the following areas:

- Age: if you are under 32 years old
- Qualifications: UK degree level or professional level qualifications (including MBA provision)
- Previous earnings
- UK work experience.

Other permits exist for temporary work in the UK. If you are a gap-year student, you may work in education in the UK for up to 12 months. You may work in other sectors for up to 12 months if you are from Japan and for up to 24 months if you are from a Commonwealth country.

Jargon buster

EEA An acronym for European Economic Area, which provides a single market for the free movement of labour and services, as well as most capital and products. It comprises all the members of the European Union and the European Free Trade Association, with the exception of Switzerland

 For details about work permits, visas and the Worker Registration Scheme, see the website of the Home Office's Border & Immigration Agency at www.workingintheuk.gov.uk.

Under the rules of the Worker Registration Scheme, some people from within the EEA must apply for a registration certificate within one month of commencing a new job in the UK. This includes nationals from: the Czech Republic, Estonia, Hungary, Latvia, Lithuania, Poland, Slovakia and Slovenia.

Employment rights in regulated sectors

Every employee under UK law, regardless of their nationality, has employment rights that are illegal to breach. In addition, if you are a worker who is employed in a regulated sector, your labour provider has a legal obligation to be licensed with the Gangmasters Licensing Authority (GLA). The regulated sectors include: agriculture, horticulture, forestry, shellfish gathering and the processing and packaging of food and drink. The GLA was created to protect workers from exploitation.

GLA licence: To obtain a GLA licence, your employer has to meet a number of minimum standards, including health and safety rules. These standards also include providing you with itemised pay slips from which only statutory deductions are made (income tax and national insurance) unless you have provided written

permission stating otherwise. You must be paid at least the national minimum wage and must be able to leave your job without penalty whenever you wish to give notice. You must never be subjected to physical or mental abuse and, if your employer provides you with accommodation, this must not have poor or overcrowded conditions.

Background checks: Before you accept work from a labour provider (this means **gangmaster** or a recruitment agency that will pay your wages), check that they are licensed with the GLA. Call the GLA directly (see box at the foot of page 144) and/or check whether the labour provider is a member of a professional organisation such as the Association of Labour Providers (ALP). The ALP is a grant-aided trade association for the agriculture, horticulture, fresh produce, food manufacturing and packing sectors. It ensures its members are kept up-to-date with all developments in employment law and adhere to industry codes of practice. Any members that do not comply are evicted from the association and reported to the GLA. The ALP contains a list of members on

Jargon buster

Gangmaster A labour provider or recruitment agency typically providing workers for low-skilled jobs in a range of different sectors from agriculture to food processing. Gangmasters normally refer to themselves as labour providers or agencies

its website, as well as a section that provides information, advice and job vacancies for workers.

You may also get advice or information about your employment rights from a trade union. You do not need to be a member to contact one. The Trades Union Congress (TUC) represents 66 affiliated unions and can provide you with further information about employment rights in one of several different languages.

Exploitation: If you feel your gangmaster or labour provider is exploiting you or is forcing you to work under unacceptable conditions, the GLA has the power to stop them. The GLA can help you if:

- You are being threatened or intimidated.
- You are being forced to work against your will.
- There are debts that prevent you freely seeking other employment.
- You are being forced to stay in accommodation.
- Your accommodation is not safe.
- You have had your passport retained.
- You are being paid less than the UK minimum wage (£5.52 for workers aged 22 and over from October 2007 – this regularly rises, so do check to see if you are owed more).
- Deductions are taken from your pay that are not shown on your payslip.

- You have had to pay a fee to get the job.
- You do not receive sick pay and annual leave entitlement.
- You are not allowed to take breaks at work.
- Your place of work is not safe.
- Vehicles you are transported in are not safe.

Any information passed to the GLA is done in confidence. If you do blow the whistle on your employer, your identity will never be revealed to them.

HEADHUNTERS

Headhunters are recruitment agents who specialise in recruiting senior executives, such as Archibald & Dutch, which places high calibre management and board level candidates into both permanent and interim roles within organisations across Europe, or Nu Star, which sources senior and middle managers for a range of sectors. They are so-called because, unlike the majority of high street recruitment agencies, they actively seek out the perfect candidate and may contact you even if you are not looking for a job.

Before the advent of the internet, headhunting drew heavily on contacts made through old school networks. Today the industry is very different. A headhunter is normally an expert in

If you encounter problems with your labour provider in a GLA regulated sector, contact www.gla.gov.uk (GLA) or else go to www.labourproviders.org.uk (ALP) or www.tuc.org.uk (TUC).

Jargon buster

Headhunter A recruitment consultant or agency that seeks out potential candidates for jobs, including those people who are not actively seeking new positions

a particular sector or geographical area, often both. When conducting a research-driven search, he or she first takes a detailed brief from the client company, which may or may not have publicly revealed that it is looking for a new senior executive. If commercially sensitive, the client company does not publish any recruitment advertising but asks a headhunter to find a shortlist of suitable candidates in secret.

The headhunter then studies the client's market to create a target list of organisations, from which individuals are identified and approached in confidence. If you are approached, the headhunter confirms suitability and level of interest with you, and interviews you as a pre-selection stage. You are then introduced to the client as part of a short-list. Most specialist headhunters also maintain long-term regular contact with potential candidates in their sector. Such contact also acts as a valuable network for the headhunter, often providing fresh leads to new potential candidates.

Headhunters are always on the lookout for people they could put forward

What should you expect from your headhunter?

- A clear indication from the outset of exactly what is on offer, including salary and remuneration package.
- Listening skills – make sure your recruiter understands your personal career aspirations and notes the companies or areas you don't want to work in. This is particularly important if they are unable to reveal the identity of the employer at the beginning of the process.

- A request for your CV and an interview before you are presented to any potential employers.
- Confidentiality and high ethical standards; for example, your CV should only be sent to potential employers with your permission and your headhunter should respect your requests, such as to be contacted only during the evenings on your home telephone number.

For a list of executive recruitment agencies, go to the **Association of Executive Recruiters** within the directory of the **Recruitment and Employment Confederation, www.rec.uk.com.** For other recruitment agency email addresses, see page 214.

for jobs, so don't feel that you should sit passively waiting for that secret phone call. If you are looking for a new executive position, it may well be worth your while making contact with a consultant that specialises in your area.

❝ However flattering the approach, try to focus on what you want and whether the timing is right for your plans. ❞

Think carefully about what is good for you. It can be incredibly flattering to be approached by a headhunter, but it could also turn your world upside down, especially if you had not been considering a move. Try not to be carried along by the excitement of new possibilities, but concentrate on what you want and whether it is the right moment for you to be considering a new job. Consider what you would do if, at the end of the recruitment process, you are not actually offered the job. Would you still be happy to stay where you are?

What next?

Recruitment agencies offer a valuable, mainly free, service for job-hunters. Although it is never wise to rely solely on an agency to find you work, it is certainly worth signing up to one or two.

1 Research which recruitment agencies work in your sector and what kind of work they could offer you.

2 Find out what services they could offer you; for example, could they help you with your CV or offer advice on what salary you could expect?

3 Consider working abroad and if it appeals, look for an agency that specialises in placing candidates in a country you are interested in moving to.

4 Remember to conduct your own job searches in addition to allowing your agency to search on your behalf.

5 Make sure that your agency doesn't forget about you.

Many agencies will try to help you prepare for recruitment processes by offering you practice aptitude tests. To learn more about recruitment testing, see Chapter 7.

Tests and presentations

If you found taking your driving test stressful and recollections of sitting your school exams are not among your fond memories, imagine doing both on the same day along with a presentation of your degree's dissertation and a job interview thrown in for good measure. Tough? That's just day one of the assessment centre, there's more like that to come tomorrow.

Can you do the job?

Gone are the days when scanning your CV for your qualifications was the only test of your skills that a recruiter would require. Welcome to the age of online psychometric tests, multiple-choice timed responses, verbal reasoning, numerical ability and many more.

TO TEST OR NOT TO TEST

In an attempt to avoid the worst case scenario, recruiters are increasingly turning to testing as a recruitment tool to help them in their bid to answer the most important of questions: are you the one? In many cases, especially for employers such as the Foreign Office, you will need to pass a series of tests before you are even considered for interview. Recent surveys by the Chartered Institute of Personnel and Development (CIPD) have shown a trend towards the increased use of tests during the selection process. In 2003, 49.1 per cent of employers tested for specific skills during recruitment. The CIPD's 2007 survey revealed that this had risen to 80 per cent.

Tests range from psychometric assessment for which there is no right and wrong answer, to timed essays designed to test your ability to articulate yourself. In between are myriad multiple choice and short answer questions designed to test specific areas of your ability. Some tests assess the way you behave under certain circumstances and others examine your key skills.

Test criticisms

Critics of testing claim the whole procedure is inherently unfair. They point out that recruitment tests rarely replicate what it is like to actually do the job and are weighted in favour of people who know how to succeed in tests, rather than someone who may be the best person for the job. Further arguments maintain that recruiters risk missing out on potentially excellent candidates who may have just had a bad day.

The **magic circle** international law firm Slaughter and May famously eschews any hint of testing during the recruitment of its graduate trainees. If you apply for this scheme, you will only need to submit a CV and, if invited, attend an interview. The firm asserts that the qualifications

 Aptitude tests are explained on pages 151-3, group exercises on pages 154-7 and specific skills and personality tests are looked at on pages 157-9.

listed on your CV are enough to prove your intellect and that the whole point of the trainee scheme is to teach you all you need to know about corporate law. Other areas that need to be assessed, such as your commitment and enthusiasm, and whether you will fit into the firm and be able to communicate with its most valued clients, can be tested in an interview. This is a two-way process with two of the firm's partners and is an opportunity for you to find out more about the firm, as well as giving the partners a chance to assess you. This is in direct contrast to each of the other four magic circle firms that all contain an element of testing in their graduate recruitment processes.

Test support

At the other end of the spectrum you will find employers, such as the Civil Service, who swear by recruitment tests. To join the fast track of the Government Economics Service you will be given a set number of days in which to submit an online application form and complete several online tests comprising verbal reasoning, numerical reasoning and a competency questionnaire. If you pass these stages, you will be invited to a half-day session at an **assessment centre** where you will have to complete five exercises designed to test your economic ability.

Pass these and you will be invited to a further half-day assessment where you will be further tested on your numerical and verbal reasoning and asked to complete an **e-tray exercise**. If you are still in the running after all of this, you will attend a full day session at the assessment centre. Details about what this comprises are not revealed to

Assessment centres

Assessment centre is a term applied to the use of a variety of different tests and presentations. They can take place in the employer's own offices or in an alternative venue such as a conference centre or a hotel. They are one of the fastest growing selection methods. Assessment centres can use a variety of different techniques, but most will include a mixture of the following tasks:

- Group tasks
- Group discussions
- Presentations
- Case studies
- 'In-tray' exercises
- Role-plays
- Interviews
- Written tests.

Jargon buster

Assessment centre A group of activities and tests normally held at an employer's office or in a hotel
e-tray exercise A recruitment test that asks you to organise your electronic in-box (your e-tray), delegating, referring up and dealing with tasks against the clock. You will normally be asked to explain the decisions you took during a follow-up session
Magic circle A term regularly used to describe London's top five international corporate law firms

candidates until they are invited. Finally, if you have applied for a position with the diplomatic service, you will need to go before the final selection board. Insisting on such a battery of tests is one way to ensure that all of the applicants really want the job. After all, you'd have to be pretty committed to endure such a gruelling schedule of tests, especially if you had recently graduated and had only just put finals behind you.

♪ **Practise aptitude tests and presentations to make sure you go in with confidence.** ♬

HOW TO PREPARE

The best way to prepare for a day at an assessment centre or for any aptitude tests (online or in person) is to get practising. The more aptitude tests you do, the faster and better you'll get. The more presentations you give, the more articulate you will become. And if you arrive at an assessment centre with the confidence of someone who knows what's in store and how to handle it, you'll find any interview or presentation tasks easier to do too. Treat the testing day as you would your exams. Try to get a good night's sleep and, if you have to attend an office or assessment centre, leave yourself plenty of time to get there so that you don't arrive late or stressed.

- Remain friendly and polite to the other candidates no matter how they act towards you. Very occasionally 'moles' are placed among the other 'candidates' to watch how you react to provocation.
- In group exercises, visibly contribute to the group's activities and helpfully interact with other members; throw in ideas, draw others into the exercise and keep track of the time.
- Do not dominate group discussions or dismiss other people's ideas.
- When leading a group task, involve the entire group, delegate and make strong decisions.
- When presented with a lot of information, take time to skim it before looking at anything in detail.
- Do your best to complete tasks within the time allowed.
- If you eat lunch with your recruiters, remember that they are still continuing to observe you, even if these times are not officially part of the assessment process.

The tests

As with all exams, in addition to needing to know the answers, you will do better if you have mastered the techniques. The best place to start is by having a good idea of what may be asked and how to answer it. Here are some examples to get you going.

APTITUDE TESTS

An aptitude test is the title given to verbal reasoning, numerical reasoning and abstract reasoning tests, which look at your logic and analytical abilities.

Verbal reasoning

In a verbal reasoning test, you are usually presented with a passage of text and a list of statements relating to the text. You will then be asked whether the statements are 'true', 'false' or 'can't say', based on the information provided in the text. You normally have a set period of time in which to complete this test. Verbal reasoning tests can be completed online, or with pen and paper or at a touch screen computer at an assessment centre.

Numerical reasoning

In a numerical reasoning test, you are often asked to find the correct answer to a number of questions relating to a table of statistics or a results chart. Some

testers allow you to work out your answer with pencil and paper or a calculator. Some do not.

Abstract reasoning

Tests involving abstract reasoning (or inductive reasoning) assess your ability to apply logic when interpreting a diagram. A common way of doing this is to present you with a series of diagrams that form a sequence. From a selection of further diagrams, you have to choose which best represents the next logical step. Alternatively, you will be shown a series of related shapes. You will have to choose the shape from a selection that best fits the illustrated relationship.

Spatial test

This will be a breeze if you have ever assembled flat-pack furniture, for you are presented with the flat pattern of a three-dimensional object and asked to choose which diagram best illustrates how it would look when assembled.

 An example of a verbal reasoning text is given overleaf on page 152 and a numerical reasoning test is given on page 153. For examples of abstract reasoning and spatial tests, go to the website www.psychometric-success.com.

Verbal reasoning test example

The common name for the *Tursiops truncatus* is the bottlenose dolphin, although it is also known as the grey porpoise, black porpoise and cowfish. Bottlenose dolphins can vary greatly in size, shape and colour and are often confused with other dolphins such as spotted and humpback dolphins. Bottlenoses, like many other whales and dolphins, tend to live in family groups called 'schools', which may comprise anything from two or three dolphins, to 500. Sometimes families team up with other families and provide support for each other. Bottlenose dolphins are found off all the continents except Antarctica. It is rare to see them any further north than the United Kingdom or any further south than New Zealand.

A = True: the statement follows logically from the information or opinions contained in the passage.

B = False: the statement is logically false from the information or opinions contained in the passage.

C = Can't say: you cannot determine whether the statement is true or false without further information.

Relating directly to the passage above, please answer A, B or C to each of the following statements. Only one answer is correct for each statement.

1 Bottlenose dolphins live in schools with cowfish and grey porpoises.
2 Bottlenose dolphins are rarely found off South America.
3 Offshore bottlenose dolphins tend to be rounder and fatter than those that live onshore.

Answers: 1 = true; 2 = false; 3 = can't say

How to answer: The best way to answer these questions is to read through the text once first and then tackle each question in turn. Quickly re-read the sentence or short section of text that relates to the question to double-check your answer. If you know something about the subject already, put everything you know out of your mind, as your answers must relate only to the passage before you. If you don't know the answer, don't waste time considering it, for you may run out of time and miss out on answering several more questions while you consider the one you are stuck on. Never leave a question unanswered. Even a pure guess will, in this instance, give you a one-in-three chance of hitting the right one. Leave it blank and you have no chance.

Numerical reasoning test example

Relating directly to the table, please answer A, B, C, D or E to each of the following statements. Only one answer is correct for each statement.

Chocolate consumption

Chocolate	Consumers (millions)		Percentage of consumers eating chocolate in Yr 3	
	Year 1	Year 2	Adults	Children
White	2.9	4.6	15	26
Milk	17.8	19.3	24	24
Dark	18.1	18.2	34	3
Mint	1.5	1.7	3	1
Orange	3.6	2.9	9	2

1 Which type of chocolate was consumed by more children than adults in Year 3?
   A = White   B = Milk   C = Dark   D = Orange   E = Can't say

2 How much White, Dark and Mint chocolate was consumed in Year 1?
   A = 24.5   B = 52   C = 22.5   D = 22.2   E = Can't say

3 How much Orange chocolate (in millions) was consumed by adults in Year 3?
   A = 11   B = 2.9   C = 17.5   D = 9   E = Can't say

Answers: 1 = A; 2 = C; 3 = E

How to answer: Pay close attention to the questions, for many of the answers have been cunningly designed to try to catch you out.

For example, your addition may be spot on, but if you have added up column 1 when the question actually applied to column 2, you'll be marked down. As with the verbal reasoning, never leave a question unanswered.

"Some of the questions are designed to catch you out, but never leave a question unanswered."

GROUP EXERCISES

Many group exercises employ role-play techniques, where you are asked to demonstrate how you would deal with a particular situation. By placing this in a group context, in addition to showing how you would solve a problem, you also demonstrate how well you interact with other people and how good you are at working in a team.

❝ Putting role-play into a group exercise tests how well you interact with other people, as well as your problem-solving skills. ❞

Group role-play example

ABC Ltd is extremely busy and as Team Leaders you have been left in charge while Myles and Nadine attend a presentation. Before they went they left a list of tasks for you to do.

It is the 28th of the month. Your team has not made its targets this month. This is because you are one person down due to sickness and other situations have occurred during the month that you have had to deal with.

Working together, discuss and prioritise the list below and give your reasons for the choices you make. You have 15 minutes to present your choice.

List

- Provide end-of-month sales figures for Nadine.
- Do a probationary review on Phyllis, who has been working for you for 12 weeks.
- Deal with three customer complaints that have come in.
- Deal with one member of your team who has burst into tears after a customer was really vicious on the phone.
- Myles has asked to ensure that three callers are put through to you to take an important message for him.
- Write the report on the success of the latest campaign.
- Choose your member of staff to be recommended for employee of the month.
- Hold a brief communication meeting and go through the points left by Nadine with your team.

Role-play

This role-play is designed to test the ability of team leaders to deal with a demanding situation, work as a team and delegate. You have to assess the situation and agree as a group on the best way to deal with it.

How to answer: What your assessors are looking for is recognition of your responsibilities as a leader and your ability to articulate this persuasively to your group. If you strongly disagree with the approach your group wishes to take, stay calm. Get drawn into an argument and you'll be out, regardless of whether you were right or not. If you find yourself at odds with the group, accept the majority decision, but make a request for your disagreement to be noted.

- **Pay close attention to the instructions.** You are told to, 'Give reasons for the choices your make.' You are also given 15 minutes for your presentation; this is a long time, requiring a considered approach. Do not just read out the list in your order of priority. This will take less than a minute and will give no indication of the thought process that brought you to your decision. Your recruiters won't look favourably on your inability to follow instructions.
- **Before you start,** agree on who should present your results. If this is you, begin by standing up and introducing yourself and every member of your group. Explain what process your group used to reach its decision; was it unanimous, majority-based, or was one member given the ultimate decision? Then explain your answers.

Your presentation should go something like this:

'As Team Leaders, we believe it is vital to respond to emergency situations immediately, regardless of the size of our in-trays. In this case one member of our team is crying following a distressing phone call. It is an absolute priority to deal with her needs first, both for her sake and for the morale of the rest of the team. We would invite her to take a time-out, in our private office, in the garden, or in the ladies' room as she prefers, so that she has the breathing space to calm down and compose herself. We would ask her to come and talk to us when she felt better so that together we could deconstruct the vicious phone call and agree on tactics for dealing with abusive customers in the future. It is important to do this immediately so that her feelings of distress are minimised as quickly as possible and are not able to interfere with her ability to do her job in the future.

❝ Remember that the assessors are looking for evidence of leadership and that you can articulate your thoughts clearly. ❞

155

'Our second task is to recognise that Myles has asked us to take three important messages for him. The calls may happen at any time, but as they are messages, they are unlikely to take up too much time. We ask the receptionist to put the callers through, no matter what, and we resolve to deal with them as they happen. If, however, we are unable to take a call for any reason (perhaps because we are already on a call talking to a customer who has complained), we have delegated Louise, our second-in-command, to take this message on our behalf.

'Next we start to deal with the customer complaints. Customer complaints can be turned into examples of customer satisfaction if dealt with properly. If we can recognise that something has gone wrong and take immediate steps to put it right and compensate the customer if necessary, the customer is likely to appreciate our prompt action. However, if we appear to ignore them, the

customer's dissatisfaction will only grow. To this end, putting things right for our customers promptly is always our priority.

'Once the customers have been pacified, the next pressing issue is to ensure the team knows what points Nadine has left for us to concentrate on. We give the team an hour's notice of the meeting so that they can finish any calls they are on and can prepare any issues they wish to bring to the meeting. During this time, we debrief our distressed colleague and complete Phyllis's probationary review. If her probationary period was three months, this time has already elapsed and her needs are pressing. It is important that this happens today and she is not made to wait any longer.

'Once the review is over, we chair the communication meeting and confirm that the team understands what Nadine wishes us to do. Any other questions are also dealt with, although we keep a tight control over the meeting and ensure that it only lasts 15 minutes.

'After the meeting we turn our attention to writing the report on the success of the latest campaign. We had flagged this success in the communications meeting and wanted to complete the write-up while the success was still fresh.

'Our final two tasks are to provide end-of-month sales figures for Nadine and to choose who should become employee of the month. It is not possible to complete the sales figures

"When giving a presentation, explain what process your group used to reach its decision. Then explain your answers. "

for there are still two more days to go before the end of the month, but we make a good start on them so that even if other issues dominate our time during the next two days, we are still able to complete the figures as the month ends.

'The final job on our to do list is to choose our employee of the month. We have left this task until last as it is the least pressurised by time. Although it would be good to announce the employee of the month on the last day of every month, it is easy to explain to colleagues if the announcement needs to be made two or three days late. In this instance, however, we still have two days before the end of the month and it is unlikely that we will not be able to complete this task by then.'

SPECIFIC SKILLS

Some tests will examine your ability to complete the tasks you will be faced with during your employment. If applying for the Government Economic Service, one of the tasks you have to do is write a policy report for a non-economist. This involves 'translating' a technical report into jargon-free English. This reflects the kind of work you may have to do in the job.

The best way to prepare for this test is to go to your economics degree textbooks and find examples of economic reports. Imagine yourself as the economics editor of the BBC. How would you present this report to your viewers or listeners? Would they turn you off for being too boring or difficult to understand? Can you think of good examples to bring the statistics or

equations to life? Your report may be on how water-wastage can affect government coffers. Bring it alive by comparing it to a dripping tap at home. How much would it cost the average household over a year? How would this relate to all the homes in the UK? How could that affect the treasury?

If you are applying for a job in office administration, such as a secretary, you may be tested on your typing speed and your ability to spot errors in a written document. How many can you find in our example letter overleaf? We reckon there are 20 of them – the answers are given at the foot of page 159.

❝ When writing a report for a non-specialist, imagine yourself as a journalist and try to think of examples to bring the statistics to life. ❞

PERSONALITY TESTS

Recruiters rarely use general personality measures such as Myers Briggs during the recruitment process. However, they do use psychometrics that test how you would approach your job and look at your motivation, talent and preferred working culture. Examples of these include the Saville Consulting Wave and SHL's Occupational Personality Questionnaires, which are designed solely for use in a business environment.

Presenting yourself

Whether feeding back from a role-play or standing up before an audience complete with a PowerPoint presentation, it is likely that you will have to present yourself at some stage of your recruitment or your career.

PRESENTATIONS

There are several different types of presentations you may be asked to perform as part of the recruitment process. You might be asked to give a ten-minute speech on why you are the best candidate for the job. You may have to lead a five-minute talk on a subject you are handed 30 minutes prior to your presentation. You may have to explain why you took the decisions you did in a role-play or in-tray exercise. Whatever style of presentation you are asked to perform, the key to success lies in your preparation. Take your cue from professionals, such as actors or television presenters. Every one of them thoroughly rehearses what they do in advance. And so should you.

> **❝ When preparing a presentation, practise your body language to look relaxed but in charge. ❞**

Body language

- **Practise your body language.** Stand in front of a mirror and try different poses. Do you feel more comfortable with your weight on one leg? Do you look aggressive when you stand straight on with your legs wide apart? Try to be natural. Think about your hands. Putting both in your pockets can look a bit sloppy. How about one in a pocket and one stressing a point? This can look relaxed and in charge at the same time. Try clasping both loosely in front of you, unclasping them occasionally to stress a point with one or both hands. Practise leaning on a high stool or kitchen work surface; you may have a lectern and it is a good idea to work out how best to stand behind it.
- **Think about how your body and your voice best express what you want to say.** Don't shout, but don't whisper either. If you have learnt your presentation off by heart, you can

For more advice on body language in interviews, see pages 170–1.

What not to do

- Keep eye contact with one member of your audience for too long. It will seem like you are staring at them.
- Look down. Your voice will sound muffled if directed at the floor.
- Pace. You will seem distracted, nervous, manic, or all three.
- Argue with anyone in your audience, regardless of whether you have been heckled.
- Laugh at your own jokes. It's just not cool.
- Chew gum. Even if you are giving up smoking, it is never polite to talk while chewing.

look at your audience and build up a rapport. If you have to read from your notes, you risk sounding boring and you lose the ability to assess your audience's reactions as you will be looking at your paper rather than them. If you are nervous and holding a sheet of paper, its flimsiness can work against you by exaggerating and highlighting any tremble in your hands.

Presentation preparation

These tips on presentation preparation apply to all presentations, regardless of their length or format.

- Define the key message you want to convey.
- Decide on no more than three sub-messages.
- Prepare a definite beginning, middle and end.
- Start by introducing yourself and then make an impact with a quotation or an attention-grabbing headline. You could also end with re-introducing yourself because in that way you secure your interviewers' interest at the beginning and end with what you want them to remember: you.
- Consider a spot of audience participation; it's a great way of keeping them awake. Make sure you know what you are talking about and invite questions from your audience either during your presentation or after you finish speaking.
- Leave enough time to produce and print handouts. They should be clear and easy to follow.

Making the presentation

Many interview presentations will require you simply to stand up and talk for a set period of time on a set subject. However, some may ask you to prepare a PowerPoint or use visual aids to support your presentation.

- **If using PowerPoint,** don't simply read the slides, and try to avoid listing bullet points, this is boring. It's much better to use drawings, graphs, diagrams and photographs to illustrate your points.
- **Learn your presentation.** Practise it again and again, in front of a mirror and in front of family and friends if possible. Only use paper as a prompt sheet if you really need it and then make sure you put it down on a table, chair or even the floor rather than holding (and possibly shaking) it.
- **Take your time.** If you need to use any kind of equipment as part of your presentation, whether this is an overhead projector, a slide projector or PowerPoint-driven computer screen, ask for some time to familiarise yourself with the equipment before you need to use it. If you are not sure how to make it work, ask someone to show you in advance. The last thing you need at this time is to throw yourself off-balance by messing up on the technology.

 Technology goes wrong. Always have a back-up plan if your presentation uses technology. Rehearse delivering your presentation with no visual aids, so that you can continue, unflustered and still brilliant regardless of what the gremlins do to your machines.

- **Bring copies of the presentation with you.** If the technology blows up, you can then simply pass around handouts. Being so well prepared will certainly earn you a few points with your recruiting panel.
- **Deal with questions effectively.** When you end, ask your audience if they have any questions. If they do, repeat the question before you answer it to confirm you have heard it correctly, to ensure everyone else has heard it and to buy time to gather your thoughts.

❝ If using PowerPoint, don't just read the slides. This is boring. ❞

 If you need to brush up on your PowerPoint skills, explore courses at your local further education establishments.

SEEK HELP

Most of the best actors have attended stage school and most of the best television presenters have received training. Why should you criticise yourself for failing to achieve their standards without any help? If you are worried that your presentation technique may let you down, either during the recruitment process or perhaps later during the job itself, you may benefit from some presentation coaching.

If you are looking for a coach to help you prepare for a presentation, shop around. Ask any prospective coaches how they plan to help you and what you need to do in preparation for your lesson. Ask if they have helped anyone prepare for a job interview or presentation before and if they could supply you with any references. Try, where possible, to speak to former clients; they should be able to give the best insight into whether presentation coaching is for you.

Presentation coaching

Here are some examples of presentation trainers that are representative of the market in that most of them have experience in performance arts as well as offering support services to business and individuals.

- **Training Hand.** Delivers modular programmes or single courses designed to help people improve their communication effectiveness.
- **Voice Business Associates.** Helps clients with confidence and presentation techniques. With a background in the performing arts, linguistics, voice therapy and business facilitation.
- **Voiceworks.** General courses or tailored training to help people with a range of public speaking.

> **❝ Presentation coaching can be beneficial if you are worried about your technique. It can help you to raise your standards. ❞**

Websites for the coaching companies are: Training Hand (www.traininghand.co.uk), Voice Business Associates (www.voiceba.com) and Voiceworks (www.voiceworkslondon.com).

What next?

At some stage in your career and life, if not in your recruitment, you will need to perform a presentation or speech. Good performers are made, not born, so think about this in advance and then prepare and rehearse. The same principles may be applied to tests. Understand what you need to do in advance and then practise.

1 Find out if your prospective employer uses tests during recruiting and, if so, what kind.

2 Research practice papers and do as many as you can.

3 Think about speed and do them against the clock.

4 Prepare possible presentations. Think about your body language and your voice.

5 Watch news and documentary television programmes for examples of how people present and stress points.

6 Rehearse, rehearse and rehearse again.

7 If necessary, seek professional help.

Many assessments and presentations take place on the same day as your interview. For tips and advice on how to prepare for your interview, read on.

The interview

In an interview, employers are using an increasingly complex variety of techniques to separate the maybes from the definites. From an informal chat over lunch to a grilling by a six-strong panel, there are many approaches and a seemingly infinite list of questions. Of these, the one you need to consider first is, are you ready?

Interview preparation

As with any test, exam or challenge, a vital key to success lies in your preparation. If you are ready for it, you can handle almost anything. If you're not ready, it will be painfully apparent to all who are watching.

Congratulations! You have made it through to the interview stage. Whatever happens next, from your interview preparation, to the interview itself and the offer or no offer of a job, you should keep in mind that someone has been interested in you and thought, on paper at least, that you have something to offer.

This is a two-way street, however. It is all very well that your prospective employer is interested in you, but are you interested in them? An interview is the perfect place for you to check them out. Can they provide what you would want from a job or a career?

It is easy to forget in the rush to get ready for an interview that you have come a long way already. The fact you have even been offered an interview should give you some confidence. Try to remember this and draw on it, as it is a

good way to allow your inner confidence (as opposed to nervousness or even abject fear) shine through during your interview. The other thing that will give you confidence in your interview is being prepared. That means taking practical steps, such as making yourself aware of what type of interview you might have, as well as more knowledge-based steps that will help you to work out how you will tackle the questions you are asked.

GENERAL INTERVIEW PREPARATION

There are many different types of interview, ranging from the formal to the informal. How you tackle each will differ slightly; however, there are several things you can do to prepare for an interview that are common to all.

Practical preparation

When you call to confirm that you can attend the interview, check the date and time. Mistakes can be made on interview invitations, confirming that you have the correct details now will save trouble and potential embarrassment later. Use the call as an opportunity to check further details, as outlined opposite.

66 Getting an interview shows you have something to offer. It also allows you to check out your prospective employer. 99

- How long the interview will last.
- If there are any group exercises.
- Who you will be meeting.
- What will be expected of you (will you have to complete any tests, for example?).
- If you have a disability, check the physical access to the premises as necessary and indicate any additional support that you might require during the interview. Your recruiter has a legal requirement to support your needs.
- Work out in advance how to get to the interview venue. Do you know where it is exactly? You should also check on routes and confirm the times of train departures and arrivals, or the length of car journeys, for example. Remember to check for any planned disruptions to road or rail services.
- Plan to arrive early to allow for unforeseen delays in your journey. The last thing you need is to arrive rushed. If you end up arriving much too early, go for a walk around the block or have a drink in a nearby café.
- If you are asked to bring certificates, references, or any other documentation, get them ready well in advance to avoid having to chase around on the morning of the big day.
- Take the interview invitation with you (it should contain the name and contact details of your interviewer, as well as any other information you may need on the day).
- Take your mobile phone. If you are running late, you can call your contact to warn them, although don't forget to turn it off before the interview.

- Take several copies of your CV or application form. You can use one as a prompt before you go in and it will also help you to appear well organised if you can supply a spare for someone who is missing a copy. Be careful to ensure that you take the same CV or form that you sent in originally.
- Whenever you are planning to meet someone you don't know, it is a good idea to tell someone where you are going and when you expect to return (if possible, leave an address and telephone number). This is good practice regardless of whether you are going on a blind date, you are a journalist preparing to meet someone for a story or you are going for an interview.
- Take enough money for an unplanned taxi ride or a drink in a café should you arrive too early.
- Take a small bottle of water to help you overcome any anxiety induced problems, such as a dry mouth or a tickly cough.

In addition to practical preparation, you will need to do some research before your interview (see the ten things to know about your employer, overleaf).

❝ Use the internet to check out the company and its competitors. ❞

Ten things to know about your employer

1 Know their products or services well. What do they offer? Study their website.

2 Their latest product launch or marketing push. Look for this in local, national or trade press and on the company website.

3 Last year's profits compared to the previous year. This information may be available on their website and will be in their annual report (just phone and ask for one). If not, for a small fee, you can see a company's financial records through Companies House (www.companieshouse.gov.uk).

4 Company ethos. A mission statement or 'who we are' section can normally be found on the company website or in their annual report.

5 The company's history. Who founded the company and when? How and why has it changed over the years? Some of this information is available from Companies House free. You could find the rest in the press and on the website.

6 The company's future. Which areas are the company looking to expand into? Have you got any ideas that might enhance the company's future? You may find useful information in the press or it may be a closely guarded secret. Be imaginative; put yourself in the employer's shoes.

7 Competitors. Who do they share the marketplace with? What are their strengths and weaknesses by comparison? The internet is your best source for this information.

8 Negative press. Has the company been in the news recently? Search individual press archives or go through a news portal such as Google News.

9 Positive press. Has the company had any successes in addition to product launches or profits? Do they promote a charity or have they won any awards? Check out the press, but also look on the company website, they're likely to promote positive news about themselves.

10 Company personnel. Who are the main players? Has there been a radical change in leadership? Search press archives, the company website and their press release.

> A vital focus of research is yourself. If your potential employer has done the same, at least you'll know what kinds of things they may have found out about your netrep and can prepare your defence if asked in interview. If you're quick, you can remove awful things before they're seen.

application form and have a few extra besides. Make a list of five adjectives that best describe your professional strengths and provide a positive example for each.

- **Check your contract** for your notice period; your interviewer may ask how much notice you need to give your current employer.
- **Think about whether you have any holidays booked.** Your interviewer might want to know this, so you should be prepared to provide dates.

Question preparation

- **Prepare for a wide range of questions.** Don't just consider standard interview questions (though you will need to think about these too), but investigate a range of things your interviewer may ask you and how you can best reply. And that means thinking about tricky questions too.
- **Prepare a handful of your own questions to ask.** If you can think of five good ones, it will give you a few options if some of them are answered during the course of the interview anyway.
- **Know yourself and review your accomplishments.** Think of specific examples and anecdotes that illustrate your strengths. Be ready to expand on the points you made in your CV or

❝ Be ready to handle a wide range of questions, and have some of your own to ask. ❞

PHYSICAL AND PSYCHOLOGICAL PREPARATION

You know where you are going and you know what you are going to say, but that is not all you need to do in preparation for your interview. You also need to think about how you are going to behave. If your nerves get the better of you and you become a fidgeting, incoherent shadow of yourself, your interview will not be as good as it could have been. Take steps to calm yourself and give a

For a range of real interview questions, turn to pages 178–91. When thinking about your interview, prepare answers to them.

boost to your confidence. This also means paying attention to what you look like. If you look good, you'll feel good.

Attitude

Psychologists have proven that if you can visualise success, you are more likely to experience it. This is a phenomenon widely exploited by sports professionals, but there is no reason why it could not work in a situation such as an interview. See yourself in the interview as calm, positive and confident.

Appearance

Prepare what you are going to look like, which means making sure you are clean as well as choosing your wardrobe. Check your fingernails. Your interviewer will want to shake your hand and if your fingernails are dirty, it won't make a good impression. You should also not wear an overpoweringly strong perfume or aftershave.

Choose suitable clothes. Your potential employer will probably want to choose someone who appears to fit in. If you wear clothes that look appropriate for the organisation, you will give the impression of fitting in nicely. A creative agency may not feel so comfortable about interviewing a candidate in a classic 'city suit' as a corporate would. But whatever you wear, make sure you make an effort and don't dress casually. If you are

unsure what to wear, do a bit of homework and 'doorstep' the firm. What are the staff wearing? If they are smart, follow their lead, though err on the conservative side and avoid a novelty tie or low-cut dress. If the staff are casual or in uniform, go for smart. Most interviewers expect candidates to make an effort for the interview, even if normal day-wear at work will comprise jeans and tee shirts.

Body language

If you don't feel comfortable about your body language or your communication skills, practise them. Sit in front of a mirror and try smiling over and over until you have captured a grin that both feels and appears natural, easy and pleasant. Try to avoid sitting stiffly with folded arms, or slouching back in your chair. The former can be interpreted as pent-up aggression or too much anxiety, depending on the other visual clues you give out. The latter is far too relaxed for an interview and may be interpreted as lazy or arrogant.

- Your best posture is to lean slightly forward. This gives the appearance of being interested in the conversation.
- Look your interviewer in the eye, but break off eye contact too. If you don't, you might come across as a little weird and intense.

 There are plenty of books available on the subject of body language: search on www.amazon.co.uk or ask your local bookseller.

- Use your hands to express a point (don't flap them about though), and nod occasionally while listening to show you agree.
- Concentrate on your voice. Try to avoid speaking too quickly or mumbling. If you need a moment to think, don't panic about it, but just take a sip of water to buy you time or simply say, 'Hmm, let me think about that.'

You probably do all of these things without thinking, but if you feel really nervous about the whole prospect of interviewing or presenting, consider signing up to a coaching agency. Many of these are run by actors, who can give great tips on how to best present yourself (see page 163 for further information about coaching).

If you are beginning to get really nervous about the prospect of the interview, try some relaxation techniques. Be true to yourself; think about what makes you relax personally. There is hardly any point trying to meditate to the sound of whale song if the whole exercise makes you want to throw your CD player out of the nearest window. Avoid too much caffeine before the interview (tea, coffee and cola), as it is a diuretic, and remember to pop to the loo before you go in. The last thing you need is to feel like you are bursting to go in the middle of the interview.

❝ Find a way to relax that works for you, and avoid too much caffeine before the interview. ❞

Body language and your interviewer

- Body language works both ways. If your interviewer can 'read' your body language, you can also read theirs. Use what you see to your advantage.
- People like people they can relate to. If you copy some nuances of the interviewer's behaviour, on a subconscious level at least, they are more likely to see you in a positive light. So, if your interviewer speaks slowly, speak slowly too. Take care not to overdo this, it may appear you are mimicking them.

- Respond to your interviewer's buzz words. If your interviewer uses terms such as:
  - dynamic
  - energetic
  - go-getting or
  - aggressive
  it will indicate that he or she feels a sense of urgency about your role. Respond in kind by acknowledging that you feel the need for speed when approaching a named element of the job.

Types and styles of interview

There are many different types and styles of interview. The kind you encounter will largely be dictated by your circumstances or by the job that you're applying for, as well as the personal preferences of your own interviewer.

TYPES OF INTERVIEW

From talking to an individual on the telephone, to facing an interrogatory panel, you may find yourself in many different types of interview; sometimes for the same job. Although you will still need to complete your general interview preparation, you will also need to think about some special issues that affect each type.

Telephone/videoconference/webcam

Most commonly, telephone interviews are used as part of the initial method of screening candidates. This is especially true if candidate and interviewer are located a long way away from one another, or are in different countries. If a company has multiple or international offices, you may be invited into your closest office to be interviewed via their videoconference or webcam facilities. In these instances, you would normally be accompanied by an employee who is trained to use the equipment and will provide you with some 'human contact'. Treat these types of interview exactly as you would an in-person encounter and read up on the firm.

If you are taking part in a telephone interview, it can be helpful to have some notes to hand. If you have provided your mobile number as your primary contact, make sure you keep it well charged at all times and try to take the call in a place where you will not be disturbed. Speak slowly and clearly, there is no need to rush your answers.

If you are taking part in a webcam or videoconference, remember that, unlike telephone interviews, you still need to think about your appearance.

One-on-one

This is one of the most common types of interview and involves one person, usually a company or department boss or a senior HR executive. Depending on the job and the organisation, the interviewer will make the decision about whether to take you on or in discussion with other colleagues after the interview has ended.

Sequential or multiple

A sequential interview comprises several interviews in turn, normally over the course of a single day. Each interview is conducted by a different interviewer or panel of interviewers. The first may be a screening interview with the personnel manager or supervisor. The second may be with the person who will be your boss.

Normally each interview takes a different approach and you will be asked questions of a different nature. However, if you find you are asked the same questions again, make sure you always answer as fully as you can, although avoid repeating yourself word-for-word. Use different examples in each interview. Your current interviewer may not have heard the answer you gave in your first interview, but will compare notes with your previous interviewer.

Panel

Panel interviews are common in the public sector and in areas such as education. A panel commonly numbers three or four people, but can comprise anything from two to ten or even more. Try not to be put off by encountering a wall of different faces. One person will normally chair the panel and manage the structure of the interview. If the panel is not too numerous, try to remember everyone's name, or at least their role. The reason why there are several people is that they will probably represent a different area of the organisation. In education, for example, you might be interviewed by:

- The headteacher
- Deputy headteacher
- Senior management team teacher
- Chair of the governors
- Chair of the governors' personnel committee.

A corporate panel may be made up of the head of a division, the head of the department you are applying for and a senior HR executive.

Address your answer to the person asking the question, but try to acknowledge the others at the same time. Don't be alarmed if notes are taken, this is normal. If you can remember what each person does, you can direct questions to the appropriate person when requested to do so. At the end of the interview, shake hands with all the interviewers in turn.

> **❝ If the panel isn't too large, try to remember everyone's name and then address your answer to the person asking the question. ❞**

Group

You may be invited to join a group interview. This is where you are invited to join several other candidates and are interviewed by either one or, more often, several interviewers, or asked to take part in a group exercise on which you are assessed. Many industries use group activities (as part of an assessment centre or in their own right) to assess a candidate's ability to communicate within a team. These include, in particular, many graduate vacancies in financial services and retail. If you are required to take part in a group interview, it is normal that you also have the chance to take part in a one-on-one or panel interview too. However, group interviews can also be sometimes used as a screening method and you may not get the chance to be seen alone.

The main point of a group interview is to determine how well you act in a group situation. They are also often used when there is more than one position vacant. The interviewer normally starts the process by sparking a discussion. However, you and your fellow candidates may be asked to solve a problem collectively (although this approach tends to be used more in recruitment tests, examined in greater detail in Chapter 7). Or you might be asked to discuss your personal qualifications in front of the other candidates.

- Try to treat everyone with respect and remain cool and calm at all times, remembering to listen as well as talk.
- Avoid conflict situations at all costs.
- Keep an eye on your interviewers and try to assess what they are looking for. If you are unsure what is expected of you, ask for clarification.
- Your interviewers are probably looking for how well you cope in a group, so try to mingle and work the room. Chat to interviewers and fellow candidates alike. Introduce yourself and ask about the person you are talking to. If you have been given a topic, discuss it. If you have not, make pleasant small talk, such as asking if their journey in was OK this morning.

"Show that you can listen as well as talk. "

Case Study Leon

Leon did well at the group interview and has been invited back to take part in a one-to-one interview next week. He got off to a good start by being warm and introducing himself to individual applicants and interviewers alike before the exercise had even begun. The group of six interviewees were asked to discuss, between themselves, their individual suitability for the job as their interviewers looked on. One member of the group immediately offered to chair the discussion and invited Leon to begin. Leon obliged, but suggested it might be a good idea for someone to take notes, so that there were recorded minutes of the meeting should they need to report back to anyone not present. He offered to take the minutes, but asked if anyone was prepared to take the notes when he was talking.

Leon was marked up for graciously acquiescing to his colleague's desire to lead the meeting (this showed ability to work in a team, there's no point having a team made up of captains with no players).

He was then given further points for having the sense to see that minutes would be a good idea and more praise still for the careful way he made the suggestion and his skill in delegating part of the job.

Out-of-office

Most interviews follow a similar format: a single person or group of people are asked questions about their suitability for a given job in a room that is shut off from the rest of the organisation. It may be a meeting room or the office of the person interviewing you. However, some interviews are conducted over breakfast, lunch or in a coffee bar. The idea is that you are able to enjoy an informal encounter with your potential boss, much in the same way as you would if you went out to dine or have coffee with him or her.

Normal rules of interview etiquette apply here, with the added burden of adhering to the correct social practices. Have the confidence to order whatever you want to eat or drink. However, it might be a good idea to avoid alcohol and dishes that are tricky to eat. If you are really unsure, simply follow the lead of your interviewer, although they would probably mark you down for a limp reply such as, 'I'll have whatever you're having.'

> ❝ If you are unsure what to do if being interviewed out of the office and in, say, a restaurant, follow the lead of your interviewer. ❞

STYLE OF INTERVIEW

In addition to there being several different types of interview, there are also several different styles, any of which may be applied to one particular type. A panel interview, for example, may follow a chronological style or may be competency-based.

Standard combined

This is the most common style of interview and combines a range of questions from standard direct ones to competency-based questions and hypothetical case studies. It normally lasts 20 minutes to half an hour.

Competency

Just like competency-based application forms, competency-based interviews ask for concrete examples of how you managed specific situations. You may be asked to explain how you overcame a problem with a client or how you helped an organisation improve efficiency. Remember that you do not have to relate your answers solely to your most recent position. Try to draw on a range of examples taken from both your professional and personal life. If you have recently graduated, draw examples from your career in education, any clubs you belong to and any work experience you may have had.

Chronological

Chronological interviews take your CV, application form or your work history as the basis for their structure, with your interviewer working through what you

175

achieved and when. Try to make this interesting. If the interview seems to focus solely on your CV or application form, try to elaborate on other areas of your experience or skills to provide a wider and more rounded picture of yourself. For example, if your interviewer asks you about your experience of running a sales team for Clear Windows, explain your role and responsibilities and add that as captain of the county's tennis team, you have leadership and team experience in other areas too.

" Try to elaborate on your experience and skills. "

Portfolio

If you work in a creative industry (you may be a graphic designer, for example), you will probably be asked to bring your portfolio along to an interview. This is normally a case of wanting to meet you in person, rather than to test your competencies. Your potential employer may also use the interview to assess how well you might cope with liaising with their clients. However, the main bulk of the interview will be taken up with going through your portfolio with you. Be prepared to talk about specific challenges that a project may have presented or how you came to choose a particular design route. Try not to dominate this process as you may go on for too long and bore your interviewer. Allow them to take the lead and respond to areas of your portfolio that they appear interested in.

Verbal test

If you are trying to get a job in a technical industry, such as IT or engineering, your interviewer may want to try to gauge the level of your skills and knowledge through a verbal test.

What not to do in an interview

- Don't arrive late.
- Don't ramble or duck out of a question.
- Don't give one-word answers; give examples of your achievements at every opportunity.
- Don't say you find it hard to work under women.
- Don't answer your mobile phone during the interview (turn it off).
- Don't become emotional, timid, aggressive or arrogant.
- Don't criticise former colleagues (your interviewer will be concerned that you may do that about their company in the future).
- Don't use jargon or acronyms to summarise your responsibilities.
- Don't argue with your interviewer.

Try to relax and just answer each question according to your own level of knowledge. Don't worry if there is anything you don't know, your potential employer may have deliberately put in a few questions that you do not need to know the answer to, just to see how wide your knowledge is. Of course, you will never survive in a technical position if your knowledge is not up to the job, so this type of interview is as much for your benefit as it is for your potential employer.

Hypothetical examples

Some interviewers will simply throw a bunch of hypothetical case studies at you and ask how you would deal with each one. There is often no right answer. The idea behind this approach is that you will be tested on your analytical ability (how well you pull the problem apart and get to the bare bones of it) and your verbal reasoning (how well you can come up with a solution and express it).

Unstructured

Don't worry if your interview doesn't appear to have a formal structure. This may be a deliberate attempt on the part of your interviewer to put you at ease by presenting an informal situation where you can simply chat about yourself, your career ambitions and your interests.

INTERVIEW MANAGEMENT

If you have sent off more than one job application, it is more than likely you will be invited to more than one interview. If this is the case, it is important that you keep tabs on who said what to whom. After a while, your memory might merge all of the interviews into one homogenous mass. To avoid this, jot down notes after each one (see box, below). In addition to helping you improve your technique in future interviews, these notes should also help you decide which offer to take.

Post-interview notes
● **Length of the meeting.**
● **Who you met, their titles and contact information.**
● **What you learnt about the company.**
● **What you learnt about the people you met (background, interests, etc.).**
● **What you noticed about the culture/environment.**
● **How closely the position matched your objective.**
● **What obstacles, if any, there are in meeting your objective.**
● **Next steps/tasks to complete.**
● **Your evaluation of the meeting.**
● **Other information gained.**

For more ideas for ways to keep on top of your interview progression, see pages 51-2.

Interview questions

Regardless of whether or not you have a good idea of what kind of questions you will be asked, it will help you to consider a broad range of possible questions and how you would answer them. At the very least this exercise should help boost your confidence.

A good interviewer should be able to gain a clear sense of whether or not you are a suitable candidate for the organisation. Answering his or her questions well will depend on your advance knowledge of the organisation, its products or services, its practice and its philosophy.

Even more important for a successful interview is knowing yourself and being able to talk fluently about your past achievements your present strengths and your aims. The interviewer wants to understand both these areas and determine how well you would fit into the overall organisation in terms of style and appearance.

Above all, listen carefully to the interviewer's questions and take time in answering. Don't feel you have to rush or be talking constantly. From time to time ask questions yourself to clarify the meaning of a question or show appropriate interest in a particular point.

66 You need to know about the organisation as well as about yourself and your strengths and achievements. 99

STANDARD QUESTIONS

Here is a selection of real interview questions that are commonly asked, along with ways you could answer them and traps you should most certainly try to avoid.

Q Tell me about yourself

What to answer: You can almost guarantee that this one, or something similar, will pop up in almost all interviews, so prepare for and it and practise it until you have it polished. You can either give an overview beginning with your most senior position and then running through your jobs and education to date, encapsulating the information in your CV, or you could ask your interviewer: 'Which part of my experience would you like me to start with?'

Open with your answer to their question and finish with the summary you have practised. Keep your speech to two minutes maximum and remember to make it sound real by volunteering examples. This will sound far more interesting than hearing you reel off a list of job titles and qualifications. And don't be thrown if your interviewer interrupts to ask you a question. That probably indicates that he or she is interested in what you are saying and wants to know more on a particular point.

What not to answer: Keep your personal life out of this. It is not an invitation to talk about your children, your pets or your divorce.

Q What are your major strengths?

What to answer: The ability to talk about your strengths is an indication of self-confidence. Pick two or three of your best features that also match up to the person specification required for the job. This could be a tangible skill, such as a qualification and experience in, say, book-keeping, or an intangible one such as patience and a love of detail. Conclude with one positive intangible that was not listed but that would be a benefit in any work situation, such as enthusiasm; something welcomed by employers and colleagues alike.

What not to answer: Although an interview is not the place to be modest, you should avoid becoming an unbearable braggart. An answer such as, 'I have so many I don't know where to begin', or listing more than five will be both unbelievable and obnoxious. Try to avoid catchphrases that will have been heard a thousand times before by your interviewer. These include:

- I'm a perfectionist.
- I'm a team player.
- I have good communication skills.
- I am a self-starter.

It is quite right that you should highlight these qualities, but try to find alternative ways of expressing them and give some solid examples.

Q Why did you leave your last job?/Why do you want to leave your current job?

What to answer: It is normal to have a variety of reasons in answer to this question, both negative and positive. For the purposes of this interview, concentrate on the positive. These may include:

- Looking for an opportunity to move your career forward.
- You were impressed with what you have learnt about the way your interviewer's company operates and were keen to join their team. (You'll probably be asked what you know and how you know it if you give this response, so be prepared to provide these additional answers too.)
- You feel that to remain ahead of your game, you must never get too comfortable and must find new challenges at least every five years. Your last employer had run out of challenges for you.
- You wanted the opportunity to work with a particular person who is a renowned leader in his or her field.

If you were dismissed from your last position, tell the truth, and try not to whine. State your case simply and reassure your potential employer that such a situation would not happen again. If this is going to be the first time you have disclosed this information, make sure you practise it out loud. Try a role-play with a friend. This will be the hardest thing you will have to talk about so if you rehearse it, you will find it easier.

What not to answer: Even if true, never say you are looking for more money. And definitely avoid articulating any feuds or disagreements that have pushed you to leave.

Q Why are you interested in our company?

What to answer: This is a key question as it will indicate to the recruiter how much you know about the company. The suggestion is that the more you know, the keener you are. Someone who is ignorant about a company may appear blasé or non-committal. Your interviewer will want someone who is hungry to impress, both within the interview and within the job.

Pick one or two of the organisation's key characteristics. Be specific. If you just give a broad answer, you risk sounding trite. You could begin by explaining you have researched several leading companies in this field, but were most impressed with this company's attitude towards a customer-centred focus that is closely aligned to your own. If you were being interviewed for a position in a school, it could be that you were most impressed by the apparent happiness of the children recorded in the Osfted report and that you were keen to join a happy school.

What not to answer: Never say that you need a job. And don't just stop after the line that you had heard it is a good place to work. It's fine to say that, but it would be better to explain where you heard it. For example, is it a commonly agreed fact among workers in the industry, backed up with a top ten placing in *The Sunday Times* Best 100 Companies To Work For? It would be fine to say that.

Q What do you hope to be doing in five years' time?

What to answer: This is a question about goals and is best answered with an acknowledgement of both long-term and short-term career goals. Short-term goals may include finding five new clients that together bring at least £100,000-worth of business to the company within a year. Long-term goals may include working in a position more senior than the job you are interviewing for here, or perhaps mentoring a graduate trainee in an area you are good at. You could also show some humility by suggesting that an important career goal is to learn from a manager you respect. Your best answer will illustrate that you have ambition and a drive to succeed within the interviewer's company.

Hypothetical questions are given overleaf, followed by trickier ones on pages 184-7. For ways of dealing with more stress-inducing questions, see pages 187-8.

What not to answer: It would be too easy to try to make a joke with some throwaway remark about being retired or a lottery winner. Even worse would be to confess some secret ambition that undermines the value of the job, such as to give it all up to live on a commune in Wales, or become a stay-at-home parent with no job at all or, perhaps worst of all, working for a competitor.

Q Why should we recruit you and not one of the other candidates?

What to answer: This is another way of asking you about your strengths. Prepare your answer by looking for what your potential employer considers essential in the job description. This question also gives you the opportunity to talk about your greatest achievement and how you hope to replicate that in this new job.

What not to answer: This is not a time for modesty, never say that you are not sure and never try to make yourself appear better by criticising others.

Q What are your hobbies and interests?

What to answer: This is your chance to show how well-rounded and interesting you are. Tell the truth, but expand on why you like a particular interest, as this tells much more about you. For example, instead of simply listing, 'Reading, cooking and skiing', explain that the passion for books that drew you to study English for your degree has not diminished and that you are currently exploring the works of some contemporary American novelists.

Say that cooking good food brings you real joy and that you love visiting farm shops at the weekend to source good local produce. And don't be afraid to admit to weaknesses in your hobbies too. Perhaps you could explain that the first time you went skiing was a disaster and you vowed never to repeat the experience. However, you felt it was a bit unfair for your partner who was a keen skier and you persevered, finding that after a few more lessons you became pretty competent and now love it.

What not to answer: Never lie. If you say you are a keen skydiver and it turns out that your interviewer really is, you risk being brought into a conversation you can't handle. For example, how would you respond if you were then asked what was your favourite airfield to jump from? If you can't think of one, you will probably be caught out as a liar and end your chances of progressing any further with the company there and then.

Q What do you think about the American presidential elections?

What to answer: Expect at least one question that canvasses your views on current affairs and issues of the day. Your interview won't be a general knowledge test but you should be able to demonstrate a general idea and understanding of what is going on in the world.

What not to answer: Be careful not to get drawn into a political discussion. It is your understanding of the events that is being tested, not your opinion.

COMPETENCY-BASED AND HYPOTHETICAL QUESTIONS

These questions provide you with an excellent opportunity to highlight your achievements and focus on your strengths. Take your time. You won't be expected to have a brilliant solution to a complex problem on the tip of your tongue. Ask if you can have a minute or two to collect your thoughts before launching into your story.

The easiest way to prepare for these questions is to think of a case study in which you have performed well. Write down a list of things your case study demonstrates. It is likely your example can be applied to several competency-based questions. So, think through these scenarios and give yourself as many options as possible for the big day.

" Try to work in a case study where you performed well. "

Q Describe a situation in which you and your manager worked well together in order to overcome some challenges.
What this question wants to find out:
- Do you respond and relate well to your bosses?
- Are you going to be easy to challenge and develop?
- Do you need minimal direct supervision from your boss?
- Do you understand what your goals and objectives are?
- Are you a problem solver?

Possible answer: Last year my manager challenged me to find new ways of cutting waste throughout my department. This was in response to a company-wide pledge to improve environmentally friendly practices and an attempt to cut costs following a new council scheme to charge companies by the volume of their waste. I was pleased he chose me for the project and was determined to show him he had made the right choice. I conducted an audit and found that the majority of our waste was caused by printed paper and polystyrene cups. With the approval of my manager, I launched a departmental campaign for staff to bring in and re-use their own ceramic mugs. I also installed paper-recycling bins at key points around the office (next to photocopiers and printers). The volume of waste produced by our office was more than halved. In response to the success of this operation, my manager is now investigating the possibility of rolling my initiative out to the rest of the company.

Q What has been your most successful experience in presenting formally, or communicating ideas to others?
What this question wants to find out:
- Do you understand how others think and work?
- Can you determine the best way to get things done with them by talking their language?
- Can you craft approaches likely to be seen as appropriate and positive?
- Can you adjust your presentation style to the audience?

Possible answer: A couple of months ago, my creative team was asked to work on the biggest pitch our company had ever gone for. As account director, it was up to me to coordinate and ultimately present the project. In addition to persuading the client that we were able to cope with such a large project, we needed to showcase our ideas to the global divisions who would be working with us. We decided to present the pitch in a creative version of the United Nations, with a multilingual show. This was partly to demonstrate how our ideas would work in the different languages and partly so that we could ensure every division truly understood what we were saying. We won the pitch and in the post-presentation feedback we were told that we had done the best pitch the company had ever seen.

Q You have an employee who wants to work part-time. Her line manager doesn't think the department can cope with the loss of hours. Show me how you would pursue a successful compromise to this disagreement.
What this question wants to find out:
- Can you step up to conflicts and see them as opportunities?
- Can you read situations quickly?
- Are you a strong, open and focused listener?
- Can you find common ground and achieve cooperation?

Possible answer: I would first talk to the employee and line manager separately to ensure I have fully understood both points

of view in the conflict. Hearing of a disagreement second- or third-hand can mean opinions and needs are distorted. I would also ask the line manager to provide me with a summary of the employee's role in the department and how her work connects to that of everyone else. I would also ask the manager how he envisages her role changing, if at all, over the forthcoming year. If this revealed that her hours really could not be cut without a negative impact on the department, I would discuss the possibility of a job-share with the employee and her manager. I think the department could manage fine with two part-time workers completing the job, but I think a greater degree of continuity could be achieved through a job-share.

❝With hypothetical questions, consider what the recruiter is trying to find out about you.❞

Q How do you keep your team motivated and informed when everyone is very busy and facing a tight deadline?
What this question wants to find out:
- Are you good at establishing clear directions?
- Can you set stretching objectives?
- Can you maintain two-way dialogue with colleagues who are under pressure and feed back information and results to them?
- Can you bring out the best in people?
- Are you a clear communicator?

183

Possible answer: If facing a possible crisis of motivation while working on a tight deadline, I would call a summit meeting for everyone on the project, stating at the outset that the meeting would take no more than half an hour. (If people are already stretched for time, I don't think they will want to be interrupted by interminable meetings.) In the meeting I would outline the work that needed to be done and the deadline when it needed to be done by. I would also outline the importance of the success of the project to the success of the company. This is to confirm that everyone knows and understands the objectives. I would then go on to explain that I understood the pressure everyone was under and appreciated the work they were doing. I would outline what measures the company was taking to alleviate the pressure on staff and would ask if there was anything else that could be done by the company. I would close by suggesting that a mini–meeting, lasting no more than ten minutes, take place at 9.30am every morning for the duration of the project so that everyone is aware of the progress of the project and can air grievances, concerns or good ideas to the group.

TRICKY QUESTIONS

The one thing all of us dread when facing an interview is being asked a difficult question that we don't even know how to start answering. The best way to overcome this fear is to actually expect some tough questions. The examples below will give you an idea of some tricky ones. But remember, you don't have to know the answer to everything you are asked. Especially if it is a technical question designed to test your knowledge; simply say if you don't know. Some interviewers may even ask you questions that are impossible to answer, just to see if you'll admit what you don't know.

Q What are your weaknesses?

What to answer: This question is best handled by picking something that you have made positive steps to redress or something that will have no negative impact on the vacancy for which you are being considered. For example, if your IT ability is not at the level it could be, state it as a weakness but tell the interviewer about training courses or time spent outside work hours you have used to improve your skills. Your initiative could actually be perceived as a strength.

What not to answer: Under no circumstances should you say, 'I don't have any weaknesses', for your interviewer won't believe you. 'I have a tendency to work too hard', will be seen as avoiding the question.

 The answer to the group role-playing exercise on pages 155-7 gives you more of an idea as to how to present yourself and your decisions in a positive light.

Ten ways to present your weaknesses as positives

1 Impatience. Explain that you have little patience for sloppy work.

2 Languages. If ability in foreign languages is not needed for your job, explain how you always wanted to speak more fluently when abroad.

3 Obsession with detail. Reveal you have a tendency towards fastidiousness.

4 Ruthless. When it comes to winning a pitch or a new client, you can be ruthless.

5 Nervous about public speaking. Explain how you are aware of this weakness and have joined an amateur dramatics society with the intention of working on your fears.

6 Handwriting. Admit that your handwriting is as bad as a doctor's but that you have recently bought a fountain pen and intend to practise key strokes.

7 Practical tasks. If you are seeking a position in senior management, you could confess that you don't know how to change the toner in your printer or some similar more menial task that would normally be delegated to someone more junior.

8 Maths. If you are applying for a job where a head for figures is not necessary, such as journalism, admit you are weak at sums.

9 Spelling. If you are applying for a job where spelling is not necessary, such as a retail assistant, admit you are weak at spelling.

10 Competitive. Confess to having an inbuilt need to do better than everyone else, though temper this by explaining that you try to get much of it out on the squash court.

Q What salary are you seeking?

What to answer: You can prepare for this by knowing the value of someone with your skills. Try not to give any specific numbers in the heat of the moment as this could put you in a poor position when negotiating later on. Your interviewer will understand if you don't want to discuss this until you are offered the job. If they have provided a guideline salary with the job description, you could mention this and say it's around the same area you're looking for.

What not to answer: Don't give a ridiculously high figure, don't shrug and mutter whatever you'll give me, and don't say you have no idea.

> **❝ Regardless of what the issue is, refer to it lightly and dismiss it as being part of your past and not your future. ❞**

Q If you were an animal, which one would you want to be?

What to answer: Okay, this is a pretty cheesy question and the challenge will be to find a way to answer it without being cheesy. Luckily, this type of question is not very common, but it can appear in interviews for marketing and sales positions. You may also find it is a device commonly used among marketers when preparing a product for launch. For example, 'If this eau de cologne was a car, what car would it be?' The best way

to answer it is to think of an animal that is commonly perceived as portraying or representing certain qualities. These are your key. For example, you could describe yourself as loyal, intelligent and quick-witted, like a sheep dog.

What not to answer: Don't dismiss the question as being ridiculous. Although the scenario may be a bit far-fetched, it is a great opportunity to describe yourself in a really positive way. Use the opportunity positively instead of criticising your potential employers, who may not respond well to your attitude.

Q Are there any issues concerning your possible employment with us that you would like to discuss?

What to answer: If you had raised an issue on the application form or in your covering letter that you said you would prefer to discuss it in person, your interviewer might say: 'What do you mean when you write "please contact me for further details" next to the question marked "reasons for leaving your employment" on the application form?' This is your chance to explain the difficult point in your history that you have been dreading talking about. This advice is also applicable if the interviewer asked you, 'Can you explain these apparent gaps in your employment history?'

Regardless of what the issue is (a sacking, a criminal record, repeated sick days perhaps), refer to it lightly, dismiss it as being part of your past and not part of your future, and assert that your referees will be a testament to your character and

Any more questions?

It's impossible to list every question and answer you may encounter. But here are a few more questions to provide some food for thought.

- This is a large company, how will you make your voice heard?
- If a manager asked you to do something you disagreed with, what would you do?
- You need a report from a colleague by this afternoon, but they are not cooperating, how can you solve this?
- You have just received an angry phone call from a client shouting about your failure to complete a job that was not part of your brief. How should you respond?
- Do you think you will fit in here? Why?
- How would you develop talent in your team?
- What would be your first priority upon taking up the position?
- What was the last book you read and how did it affect you?
- What type of people do you get on with best?
- Do you make mistakes?

your work ethic. This could be the make or break part of your interview, so make sure you rehearse it. If available, seek advice from an agency such as Tomorrow's People, Jobcentre Plus or NACRO. An expert from the agency may be willing to hear you rehearse and should be able to offer you advice on how to tackle such issues in an interview.

What not to answer: Don't lie and don't deny that you have anything to discuss. You will be found out and have any hope of employment dashed as a result of your dishonesty.

STRESS-INDUCING TECHNIQUES

There has been a fashion, particularly with careers that are regarded as high stress such as investment banking, for interviews to be deliberately uncomfortable for interviewees. The idea is to gauge how an individual may act under pressure. The ethics and value of such an approach have been widely questioned and these types of interviews tend to be rare today. Here are some examples of what stress techniques could include and how to deal with them.

 For details on how to contact Tomorrow's People, Jobcentre Plus or NACRO, see Useful Addresses on pages 211–14.

The interviewer doesn't say anything to you for the first few minutes

Recognise this is a game and rise above it. Simply say hello and introduce yourself. If there is no response, ask the interviewer if he or she would like you to talk a little about your skills and qualities. If there is still no response, simply give a speech about what you think are your strongest features. End your speech by asking if he or she has any questions. If there is still no reply, explain that you have some questions you would like to ask about the company and you would be grateful to know if there would be an opportunity for you to ask them. If there is still no response, although it is unlikely that this would go on for so long, say thank you and offer your hand to shake. If there is no movement, simply ask if they would like to shake hands before leaving. If the interviewer is unresponsive throughout the entire exchange, ask yourself if you really want to work in this company.

The interviewer is reading a newspaper when you enter the room

Begin with the words, 'Excuse me,' and continue by explaining who you are and that you are there for the interview.

There is no introduction and the first question is tough

Don't be intimidated, that is exactly what the interviewer is trying to achieve. Attempts to inject some civility into the proceedings, such as through trying to

introduce yourself or enquiring after the interviewer's name, probably won't work. So, rise to the challenge and give your best answers straight back.

Your answers are repeatedly challenged

Accept any criticism levelled at you but do not let the interviewer walk all over you, as that will make you come across as weak-willed. Be both strong and diplomatic. Admit that you did not see the issue in the same way as your interviewer, and say that you find his or her ideas thought-provoking.

❝ Faced with a silent interviewer, introduce yourself and ask if he or she would like you to talk about your skills and qualities. ❞

COPING WITH A POOR INTERVIEWER

Most interviewers for large companies will be trained in interview techniques and, especially if they are responsible for recruiting high numbers of new staff, will probably be experienced. However, this is not always the case and you may encounter an interviewer who does not seem to be bringing the best out of you. If this is the case, you will need to take charge of the interview. Be polite but firm. Use expressions such as, 'Let me tell you about my experience in managing others', or, 'I'd like to tell you about when ...', or, 'I know this firm is keen on a hands-on approach. This echoes my own ethos, for example, I ...'

Alternatively, if the interview seems to be coming to a close and you haven't revealed your best bits, you could take the opportunity when asked for questions, for example, 'I do have some things I'd like to ask you about this company; however, before I do I would like to highlight one other area of my skills we have not touched on.' If you are not asked for questions and the interviewer is thanking you for your time and beginning to stand up, say something like, 'I see we are nearly done, but I wonder if I could just let you know about some of my skills that I feel are relevant and we haven't talked about. I was also hoping I might be able to ask you a couple of things about the company.'

ILLEGAL QUESTIONS

To remain on the right side of the law, recruiters must not discriminate on the grounds of gender, race, religion or philosophical beliefs, sexual orientation, age or disability. You should not be asked about your age, unless there is a genuine occupational requirement (the armed services and the police have minimum age requirements and you may not serve alcohol in a pub under the age of 18, for example).

If you feel uncomfortable about a particular question or line of questioning, you could say, 'I'm sorry, I'm not sure how to answer that at the moment, could we move on to the next question?' If you feel uncomfortable about the direction the interview is heading, you do not need to stick it through to the end. Be polite, but firm. Explain that you feel it is time to end the interview and leave.

❝ If you feel uncomfortable about a line of questioning, ask the interviewer to move on. ❞

Questions you should not be asked

- Are you married?
- Are you planning to start a family soon?
- What are your childcare arrangements?
- Do you have you any health problems; this job is very stressful?
- What is your religion?
- Which political party do you support?
- Are you a member of a trade union?
- Are you gay?

If you feel that you have been discriminated against, you can seek advice with your careers adviser if you have one at school, college, university or Jobcentre Plus. You can also speak to an adviser at the Citizens Advice Bureau or contact the Commission for Equality and Human Rights (see page 211). If you feel your safety has been compromised, you could speak to your union, or any union representing the industry your interviewers work in, or you could contact your local police station.

QUESTIONS FOR YOU TO ASK

During the interview, you will usually be given the opportunity to ask questions of your own. If these questions are intelligent, thoughtful and relate to the job, they will count very much in your favour. If your mind is a blank and you can't think of anything to ask, it will appear that you are not that interested in the organisation. So, make sure you prepare at least five questions. You'll only need two or three, but preparing a few extra gives you a chance if some of them are answered during the course of the interview. Whatever you do, do not ask a question that has already been answered. At best you'll look a fool, at worst it will

❝ Asking intelligent, thoughtful and relevant questions will count in your favour. Prepare them in advance. ❞

appear that you have not been paying attention during the interview.

You should be able to think of more specific questions as you do your pre-interview research on the company. For example, if the company promotes a 'green' image, you could say that you know the company has a strong waste management policy, but were interested to know of any other environmentally friendly initiatives the company adhered to. If this is something you think they are proud of, the interviewers will probably enjoy answering the question.

Ask questions about things that matter to you

Also, don't forget that you are interviewing your prospective employers as much as they are interviewing you. Don't be afraid to ask about things that matter to you. If career progression is something you care about, ask about it. For example, you could say, 'Does the company have a policy for professional development?' It is fine to take your list of questions into the interview to act as a prompt, especially if your main ones have been answered. A natural way to introduce your list would be to say, 'Well, I wanted to ask you about your aspirations for me and how you see me progressing in the company. But I am happy that we have discussed that already, so I'd just like to refer to my list to check on the other things I wanted to ask.' Try to stick to a maximum of three questions and remember to thank your interviewers for their time at the end of the interview.

Questions to ask your interviewer

66 What are the company's strategy and development plans for the future? 99

66 Are there any areas that could be a threat to the success of this strategy, both within and outside the company? 99

66 What aspirations do you have for me at the company? 99

66 To whom will I report? How would I fit into the team structure? 99

66 Are there any particular challenges associated with this job? 99

66 How is the department perceived by the rest of the company? 99

66 How do you see the successful candidate progressing within the company? 99

66 Why has the position become available? 99

Questions not to ask your interviewer

66 Why is your company seen as a poor performer in comparison to your rival? 99

66 What time is it? 99

66 What will my salary be? 99

66 How much notice do I have to give when I want to leave? 99

66 What is the recruitment procedure at your rival company? 99

The aftermath

Successfully completing your first interview is often not the end of the story. Still to come may be follow-up interviews, salary negotiations, job offers, rejections and even debriefing sessions.

SECOND INTERVIEWS

Most employers will tell you when they invite you for the first interview if there will be any follow-up interviews. In this case, the first interview may act as another level of the selection process filtering out some more unsuccessfuls, or all interviewees are invited to both, with each having a different focus. The first might concentrate on your skills and the second on your ability to fit into the company. However, there may be occasions when a decision cannot be reached after the first interview, perhaps because two recruiters disagree about who should be taken on. In these instances, you may be called to a second interview that you were not expecting.

Second interviews are very much like first-round ones apart from one important difference: you will know what to expect and, possibly, even who you will meet. You may even be given a tour of the office and introduced to potential new colleagues. Try to enjoy it. The fact that you are being asked back means your potential employer is genuinely interested in you. That's a great sign and should give you confidence. And if, for whatever reason, you are not given a job at the end, you can be sure that another employer will be equally

Second interview preparation

- Check on details such as time, date and location, much in the same way as you did for the first. Remember your second interview may not be held in the same place.
- Revise your company research notes and prepare your appearance just as you should for any interview.
- Check your notes from your first interview. Were there any areas you felt weak in? You can guarantee interview two will head straight back to these, so work on them and do more research if necessary.
- Prepare questions that relate to the first interview. For example: 'Last week, Mr Cohen mentioned the company's plan to pursue ISO 9000 accreditation. What would be my team's involvement in that area?'

interested in you and more than happy to offer you a job. Your first recruiter may even come back to you at a later date and offer you the job (perhaps the other recruit has turned it down at the last minute) or similar position.

SALARY NEGOTIATIONS

Some jobs, particularly in the civil service and public sector, adhere to strict pay scales and you will be paid according to your grade. This information is normally easy to get hold of, with either the salary figure or the grade published alongside the job advertisement. A separate section on the organisation's website, or a quick call to the HR department should reveal what price is put on what grade. Other positions have fixed figures, such as a graduate trainee scheme, for example. If you start to negotiate your salary during an interview for one of these jobs, your interviewer will be rather surprised and maybe a little put out, so it is best not to try this.

If your job advertisement does not offer a salary figure, or gives one as part of a range, you may be expected to negotiate it during your interview, or negotiate it after the interview through the recruitment agency, as appropriate. The salary range for the new role should be entirely dependent on the skills, qualities and experience required to perform that role and should not necessarily be linked to your current salary. However, if your skills and experience match the requirements of the job, then in an ideal world the salaries should be similar. This link is

likely to be less strong if you are changing careers or applying for a job that, in effect, represents a promotion from your current role.

❝ Ask for time to consider, and get the final details in writing. ❞

Salary negotiation tips

- Allow the interviewer to raise the subject.
- If your interviewer doesn't mention it, wait until the final interview and then leave it until the point you are ready to leave. Then say: 'Do you think we could discuss salary before I go?'
- Don't try to negotiate on the phone afterwards.
- If the salary range is below your current salary, but the role is sufficiently attractive, make it clear to the interviewer that you are prepared to be flexible and why you are prepared to be flexible.
- If asked about your required salary, always give a clear message that the salary is only one factor in your considerations and that others include the role itself, development opportunities, prospects and other aspects leading to career satisfaction for you.
- Once a figure has been agreed, particularly if it is lower than you hoped, ask for an early review. It is reasonable to ask for a review after six months.
- Ask for time. You don't have to agree to anything there and then. If you want to consider your options, ask to think about it overnight.
- Remember to get any final deals in writing. This can be a few days afterwards rather than there and then if need be, but don't leave it for too long.

How much are you worth?

Make sure you research what your experiences and skills are worth prior to the interview. Think about your bottom line, below which you won't go. Think, too, about whether the company is right for you and if it offers you appropriate challenges, career progression, culture, recognition and any other terms that are important to you. Don't start with your lowest figure, but don't go for a ridiculously high one either. Remember that you are talking to a potential

❝A potential employer will not respond well if they think you are playing games with them. ❞

> ### Possible benefits
>
> - **Bonus payments or incentive pay**
> - **Fuel allowance or company car**
> - **Pension**
> - **Commission**
> - **Shift allowances**
> - **Accelerated reviews**
> - **Professional society membership**
> - **Club membership**
> - **Mobile phone**
> - **Private healthcare**
> - **Overtime payments**
> - **Laptop**
> - **Share options**
> - **Insurance supplements**
> - **Tax, legal, financial counsel**
> - **Moving expenses and differentials**
> - **Membership of other company schemes such as a credit union**

employer, they won't want to feel like you are playing games with them.

Do not negotiate benefits in lieu of salary. This is because pensions, overtime rates, bonuses and salary increases are usually calculated as a percentage of you salary. Get agreement on the starting salary first, then discuss benefits and additional special considerations.

JOB OFFERS

Job offers can be made in different ways You might be offered the job there and then at the end of your interview. You may be informed by telephone, email or in writing a few days after the interview. However the offer is made, you do not have to accept immediately, or even at a By all means do accept it straight away i that is what you want to do, but it is perfectly OK to ask to consider the offer

It is best to reply to your recruiter in the same way that they contacted you (unless requested otherwise). If you wish to turn down the offer, remember to be polite and considerate. If appropriate, you could give a short reason, such as, 'I received an offer by XYZ Company, which although in many ways was similar to yours, I felt the position headed more closely in the direction I would like to go

The reason why it is important to be polite is that you may find yourself talking to the same recruiter in two years' time about another job – and for one that you want even more than this particular one. If you have been unpleasant, arrogant or offhand, you can bet they'll remember you for all the wrong reasons.

Handling multiple offers

If you find yourself in the enviable position of receiving an offer while you are still interviewing with other companies, the company that made you the offer will probably be happy to allow you some time to make your decision as long as they know what is happening and you have set firm time lines that they can agree to.

Explain that you are very interested in the offer, but need to complete your other meetings as you have already made commitments to do so. Agree on a deadline by which you will let them know your decision.

You should also let the interviewers in the other organisations know that you have already been given an offer, but that you'd like to consider their company as well. If the interview for this is not yet scheduled for another few weeks, ask if one could be brought forward for you. It might feel like a cheeky question to ask, but everyone appreciates honesty. If they are really interested in you, they will do their best to juggle your interview dates.

REJECTION

Don't despair. All is not lost. Some recruitment advisers maintain that if you get one offer for six interviews, you are conducting a highly successful campaign. Do get back on and keep applying, you will succeed eventually. However, it is also well worth stepping back and looking at where you might have gone wrong. The answer to this will depend at which stage you received the rejection.

- If it was after submission of your CV or application form, check your copies. Did you make some glaring errors that you did not spot? Check the person specification, too. Were you applying to a job for which you were not quite suited?
- If you were rejected following your interview or assessments, call the company for feedback. Most recruiters expect such telephone calls, so don't be nervous about approaching them after rejection. Whatever you do, though, don't argue with their decision. It may be that you were the second- choice candidate and if, for whatever reason, the first choice is unable to take up the position, you may still be offered the job. It would, after all, be a disaster to start a fight and ruin your excellent chances at this late stage of the process.

It is also worth remembering that you may not have done anything wrong, you could have been a brilliant candidate. But if a company had to choose one of three brilliant candidates, they would go for the person that they felt would work best in the team to which they would be assigned.

Your debrief call may remind them of how good you were and they might let you know about a forthcoming position or even one that might be available in a partner or rival firm. It is always possible to draw something positive out of a negative situation; you might just need to look for it first. So get going and start looking.

What next?

If you have applied for one of the UK's most competitive jobs, being offered an interview means you have probably already beaten several thousand people for a coveted place on the interview list. This is no mean feat, but it will be even harder to beat the remaining handful. The key to your success will lie in your preparation.

1 Prepare for your interview with both practical steps, such as double-checking the address, and your knowledge of the company.

2 Think about your body language.

3 Research different types of interviews and interview questions. Prepare your answers and how you will cope with different situations.

4 Make a list of five questions to ask your recruiter.

5 Plan your handling of job offers and salary negotiations in advance; know what you are worth.

6 Don't give up. It is normal to have several interviews before you get the job.

If you have failed to get the job, it is time to find that positive in the negative, dust yourself off and return to the recruitment merry-go-round. If you have an offer, congratulations, but don't do anything too hasty. Whatever you do, don't hand in your notice until you have a guaranteed job offer or signed a contract. For further information on how to resign from your old post and take up your new position as smoothly as possible, see Chapter 9.

The new job

Starting off in a new job can be as stressful as attending an interview and assessment centre. You will have to negotiate a raft of unfamiliar tasks, remember key details about the firm and names, appear composed and intelligent throughout while deftly outmanoeuvring any office politics. Welcome to your first day!

Unfinished business

Before you can start your new job, you will have to finish your old one. Tread carefully. How you handle this matters; it will have lasting repercussions that could affect your long-term future career.

GIVING NOTICE

In most cases, finishing your old job means handing in your notice. And as tempting as it may be to shout to your boss, 'Stuff your job Mr Smith, I'm off,' before running to the nearest exit, it is important to go about doing this in the right way. Announce your intention to leave before you have a confirmed job offer and you risk ending up with no jobs at all. End on a bad note with your current employer and you may regret it in the future when you find that the three people you upset have also moved on and are now in charge of recruitment for the only three firms you are interested in working for. And if you haven't asked already, this might be the moment you need to ask Mr Smith for a reference.

Never hand in your notice until you have received and accepted your new job's offer letter and contract. If you are only sent an offer letter, ask to read the contract before you sign anything. It may include clauses such as a **restrictive covenant**, which you will need to consider carefully and understand fully before signing. You may also have been led to believe something that is not entirely true. For example, you might be expecting a generous sick pay scheme

but discover from the contract that this does not kick in until you have been employed for a year. Read the small print and consider everything before signing and resigning.

How much notice?

If you were never given a contract, or your contract does not state your notice period, you are legally allowed to give the statutory minimum notice period of one week, regardless of your status or length of service. If this is the case and you are able to be flexible, however, allowing your employer more notice than you are required to give may help to enhance your relationship with them.

If your new employer asks you to leave before your notice period is up, you may request this from your current employer. If they say no, your new employer will

Jargon buster

Restrictive covenants Contractual obligations preventing you from competing with your current employer after you have left employment with them have to wait, unless you are prepared for a dismissal due to failing to show up for work to appear on your record.

Working your notice may seem like an arduous chore, but in fact it is a useful time for you as it gives you the opportunity to finish projects or prepare them for handover.

 If you leave without giving your contractual notice, it can affect your future references and may, If It Is noted in your contract, result in a deduction of pay to cover any loss your company suffers because of your immediate departure.

The protocol

1 First wait for a confirmed offer Including agreed salary details with your new employer.
2 Check your contract to confirm your notice period (you should have done this before your interview) and look for restrictive covenants and rules relating to bonus payments.
3 Have an informal chat with your line manager about your intentions to move on. Give good reasons why, such as trying to keep fresh by attempting new challenges.
4 Submit a formal resignation letter, announcing your intention to work your notice.
5 Work your notice. Some positions will want you to leave immediately and pay you in lieu of notice or put you on gardening leave.
6 Confirm your start date and sign your contract with your new employer.

YOUR TAX FORMS
Your **P45** shows:

- Your tax code, tax reference number and tax office
- Your National Insurance number
- When you were last paid
- Your earnings in the tax year from all your jobs
- How much tax was deducted from your earnings.

A P45 comes in four parts: Part 1, Part 1A, Part 2 and Part 3. Your employer sends Part 1 to the tax office and gives you the other three. When you start a new job, give Part 2 and Part 3 to your new employer. Keep the remaining Part 1A for your own records. Extra income is recorded on a **P11D**. Your employer only needs to declare this if you've earned at least £8,500 in the year, including the value of the benefits. They will work out how much each benefit is worth, record it on the P11D and send it to the tax

 To find your local tax office, look in the phone book or go to www.hmrc.gov.uk/local/individuals/index.htm where there is a full list of tax offices around the country.

office. They'll also give you a copy, which you'll need for your records or if you complete a tax return. If you apply for a loan or mortgage, banks and building societies will accept form P11D as proof of extra income.

TELLING YOUR BOSS

Announcing your intention to leave can be surprisingly tough. Some employers take it as a personal slight and others are annoyed at the prospect of having to recruit someone to fill your post. Many will want you to stay for these reasons, rather than genuinely valuing you. If you are asked to stay, think about the motivation behind such a request and think about how happy you would be if you did stay. Has the atmosphere soured since your announcement, is that likely to change if you stay?

Before you do anything, check your contract. Some companies have special procedures concerning how to give your resignation and to whom. All employers have a legal duty to provide employees with a contract. The best way to broach the subject is to raise it informally in

person first, followed by a resignation letter. This allows you to chat about it and soothe your manager's battered ego. Some reasons for leaving will be easier than others for a sensitive boss to take. Relocating because of your partner's work or choosing a shorter commute because of family commitments are hard reasons to argue with, they also don't suggest anything is wrong with your current job. Wanting to move on to 'something better', however, could be perceived as an insult. Explain that in order to develop, it is important for you to maximise your experience, which on this occasion means moving to a place where you can work on something completely different. Try to remain calm and gracious. It is important to maintain good relationships if you can. If your boss doesn't respond well when first told, this could be because it was a shock. He or she will probably calm down once the news sinks in.

The resignation letter

It is best to hand in your formal resignation letter the day after you have told your line manager (the person responsible for recruitment and resignations in your department) of your intention to leave. However, it is a good idea to have it to hand on the day when you reveal your news, just in case he or she demands it there and then. Your letter needs to be straightforward, brief and positive. You will also need to send a copy to your HR department or equivalent. Sending a proper letter (not an email or fax) is important as most

Example of a resignation letter

Iris Achebe
1 Market Street
London
W1 2CD

Jim Smith
ABC Ltd
1 High Street
London
W1 7EC

3 March 2008

Dear Jim

With effect from today, please accept this as formal notice of my resignation from the position of account manager.

I am, of course, happy to continue to work my contractual notice period of four weeks, which means that my last day will be 28 March 2008.

Although I am moving to a position that I hope will provide me with new career opportunities, I am sorry to leave. I have found my time with the company both enjoyable and fulfilling and would like to thank you for the support you have shown me.

Please let me know if there are any special arrangements for handing over outstanding work and responsibilities.

Yours sincerely
Iris

companies will only accept this as a formal resignation and anything else could be regarded as an example of you not showing up for work.

If you are unable or unwilling to work your notice period, you will need to request this in your resignation letter. Consider replacing the second paragraph of the letter shown on the previous page with this text:

'I understand that my contract requires me to allow for four weeks' notice. For reasons outside my control, however, I would be grateful if we could shorten this so that I could leave on 15 March 2008. I will assume that this is acceptable unless you inform me to the contrary.'

EXIT INTERVIEWS

A job offer does not always signal the end of the interview process. Many companies insist on carrying out exit interviews with employees who are planning to leave. From the employer's perspective, exit interviews are especially useful for organisations that have a high turnover. If a lot of staff are leaving, is it because the employment conditions or practices are poor? Identifying such problems is the first step on the road to rectifying them. Your exit interview may also give your employer the opportunity to gather together information from you to be passed on to your successor.

Exit interviews are also useful for you. They give you a chance to provide constructive feedback and enable you to leave on a positive note. Avoid all urges to vent your frustration or anger here. It is always a good idea to leave a place knowing that you can still return.

The interview may take place with your line manager or a representative from your HR department. It may be face-to-face or you may be provided with a questionnaire. You do not have to be forthcoming in your interview, but you should consider what this may do to your relationship.

GARDENING LEAVE

This might sound like a great idea, but it is not all about roses. Employers may only insist you serve out your notice at home if you have a clause stating so in your contract. You can't use the time to head off on holiday or even to start your new job as your employer retains the right to call you back into the office at whim. You might be asked to go on gardening leave if you are quitting a job that has access to sensitive, and especially time-sensitive, information. The idea is that by the time you have officially left, the details you were party to will have changed.

Common exit interview questions

- What is your reason for leaving?
- When did you first look for another job?
- What were the major factors that influenced your decision to start looking for another job?
- What could we have done differently that would have made you stay?
- What is your new position?
- What is your new salary?

Gardening leave is most common if you were employed in sales or a senior management position and had access to information such as client lists. If you have a gardening leave clause in your contract, you would be obliged to take it even if you feel you are not a commercial security risk. You remain an employee of the firm during this period and retain all your contractual benefits. For example, if your annual bonus came up during that period, you would still be entitled to receive it.

RESTRICTIVE COVENANTS

Like gardening leave, restrictive covenants may only be enforced if they are included in your contract and are most common for senior management positions and sales staff who have direct access to an employer's customer base, supplier prices, systems and processes. Your contract may include one of four main types of restrictive covenant. These normally only apply for a set period of time:

- **Non-compete covenant,** which seeks to prevent you from directly competing or working for a competitor, usually within a specific geographical area.

- **Non-solicitation covenant,** which seeks to prevent you from working for former customers.
- **Non-poaching of employees,** which seeks to prevent you from recruiting former colleagues.
- **Restriction on the use of confidential information,** which seeks to prohibit the use of any confidential information (usually identified by a list of examples) acquired by you during the course of your employment.

Employers don't have it all their own way, however. Some types of restrictive covenants try to impose unreasonable restrictions, which could prevent you from operating properly in your industry. Covenants are only enforceable if deemed 'reasonable' by the courts. If in doubt, seek professional legal advice.

Case Study Akin

Akin worked as a sales director for a company selling advertising space. When he took on a new position as senior sales director in a rival company, his first employer prevented him from taking customers with him to the new company with a restrictive covenant in his contract. If Akin had been able to persuade his old customers that they would be better off staying with him as he moved, it could have cost his first company a substantial amount of money in lost business.

Your first day

It is never easy starting a new job. There is a lot to learn, from what is expected of you in your new position to where the toilets are. The upheaval of change won't end until you are well settled.

Your first day in a new job will rarely see you completing a full day's work. Your time, instead, will often be taken up with completing paperwork, meeting new colleagues and learning operational procedures. Your line manager or HR manager should tell you in advance if they need you to bring in additional paperwork, such as a photograph or work permit, but remember to bring your P45, photo ID (such as your passport or a driving licence with a photo card) and your National Insurance number regardless. If you do not have a P45 (perhaps it is your first job, or maybe you lost it), don't worry. Your new employer will simply issue you with a **P46** and you will be taxed under an 'emergency code' to begin with. If this results in over-taxation, you will be compensated as soon as your tax office is able to sort it out. Many employers pay by **BACS**, where your salary is automatically paid into your bank account. To set this up for you, your employer will need a note of your bank's name, address and sort code, and your account number. It is a good idea to take these details along on your first day too. Once your details are on record, remember to check that you are

66 Much of the first day is often devoted to paperwork and learning procedures. 99

no longer being taxed under the emergency code.

BEFORE YOU START

It will help your confidence if, before you start your new job, you do all you can to increase your awareness of your new organisation. This includes:

- Re-reading the research you undertook before you were interviewed.
- Reviewing any notes you made following your interview.

- Familiarising yourself with any literature your employer sends you following their offer, such as information on products, services and technology.
- Taking up any invitations to visit the organisation prior to starting, or asking your new line manager or boss if you could stop by for a coffee and an informal chat about how you can hit the ground running.

YOUR FIRST DAY

On your first day, think about your image. You'll be meeting a lot of people for the first time, so try to pay attention to your appearance; your clothes can say a lot about your lifestyle and attitudes. In a similar way to your interview, play it safe and err on the conservative side until you are settled into your role and are more familiar with unspoken codes of practice.

You may well be nervous on your first day – don't worry, this is only natural, but try to keep it in perspective. Your new employer would not have offered you the job if they did not think that you were right for it. You may even find that some established members of staff are nervous about meeting you.

Think about your safety and wellbeing from the outset and ensure that you are familiar with first aid and safety procedures.

A good induction procedure should go through all this with you, but if not, ask. Make sure you start by listening a great deal. Try to understand where the undercurrents of office politics run and (without asking directly) if there are any office romances. (Knowing this will help you to avoid accidental tactlessness.) Be both modest and capable, and remember to exercise tact and diplomacy at all times. Try to be a 'day one' performer and get your new position off to a great start.

YOUR FIRST MONTH

In order to help you find your way around the organisation, both geographically and politically, try to establish an understanding of:

- The organisational structure.
- Who's who, both formally and informally.
- The relationship of your role to that of others.
- Communications.
- Support services available, such as IT and HR.
- Procedures and rules.
- The geographical spread of the organisation.
- The company's basic history.

If you do not already have a job description, ask for one, and then try to define as clearly as you can the boundaries of your job. You are not seeking to establish the minimum acceptable benchmarks, but frontiers within which you can make your best contribution. Do this constructively and as soon as you can.

Your job description should explain your employer's expectations of you and provide a basis for measuring your job performance. It can be used as a

Job description information

Your job description should contain the following information:
- A description of your key duties and responsibilities.
- The limits of your authority within the company.
- The resources you will have.
- Acknowledged and potential problem areas that you need to be aware of.

reference point for appraisals, training and development. It can also be used as a reference point in disputes and should help avoid arbitrary interpretations of your role by your manager. Job descriptions are often used as the basis for a company to organise your pay and grading.

When you start working in a new place, it is also worth finding out the accepted procedures and working practices (see box, below).

&& Your job description explains the expectations and how performance will be measured, and so avoids confusion over what your role is. 99

Working practice questions

- Expenses – how are they claimed?
- How do I make purchasing requests, such as for replacement of stationery?
- What welfare, sport, discount or social facilities are there and how do I obtain or use them?
- Is there an in-house newsletter (back issues can give useful information on organisation and staff)?
- Is there a union or staff association that I can join and how often do they meet and where?
- Where do people go for refreshment and meal breaks?
- Are there any notice boards?
- What are the procedures for dealing with absence requests or notifications?
- How does overtime get booked?
- Is there anywhere I'm not supposed to park?
- If I want to smoke, where can I go?

IF YOU ARE MANAGING OR SUPERVISING A TEAM

Make yourself known to your staff as soon as you can. Remember that they may feel anxious about your arrival. Encourage them and seek their advice when appropriate, but don't accept clearly wrong behaviour. For any staff you may have working for you:

- Read up on everyone's job descriptions.
- Get to know their personal histories, where possible.
- Try to understand their qualities, strengths and ambitions.
- Have an open mind and don't let a previous manager's experience influence your decisions.

Find out if there is an appraisal system and how it works. Ensure that you understand the company's procedure in dealing with issues such as recruitment, promotion and appraisals, as well as any disciplinary cases and grievances.

PROBATION

Many job offers are subject to a period of probation, which can vary between three months and a year. During this period, your assessors will be looking for confirmation that you can do the job and fulfil their criteria. Any appraisal, regardless of whether it is part of a probationary period or not, will be useful feedback for you. If you are unable to meet all of the probationary criteria, you may be asked to complete a period of additional training, or you may be dismissed.

What not to do

When you begin a new job, don't start by doing the following:

- Constantly saying how you used to do something in your last job.
- Criticising either your new or former employees or colleagues.
- Joining a clique or hitching your wagon to a star before you are sure that you have got the right one.
- Encouraging gossip or stories about your predecessor.

Areas commonly rated during a probationary review

- Technical competence.
- Relationships with colleagues and clients.
- Level of initiative and self-reliance.
- Ability to deal with problem analysis and planning.
- Time keeping and attendance.
- Progress skills to date.

What next?

Slow down! It's easy to get caught up in the excitement of a job offer. Take your time and try to leave your old employer on a good note and start your new job with terms you are happy with.

1 Wait until you have a definite offer of a new job before you tell your current employer that you are handing in your notice.

2 Follow the correct procedure for handing in your notice and do so with good grace and tact.

3 Complete your exit interview and do your best to leave on a good note.

4 Prepare for your first day in your new job as you would for a job interview, but remember to take your P45, photo identification, bank details and any other documentation that may be requested.

5 Try to learn all you can about your role and your employer from the beginning as this will help you settle into your new position more quickly and easily.

6 Avoid bad mouthing former colleagues and do your best to avoid being dragged into office politics before you have had a chance to see the fuller picture.

You've worked hard to get to where you are today, so remember to enjoy it. You have come a long way and beaten other hopefuls to get where you are. Congratulate yourself and throw yourself into your new work. The more enthusiastic you are, the more likely you are to enjoy personal satisfaction.

Glossary

Applicant tracking system Online tool designed to help recruiters monitor the progress of any given applicant throughout their recruitment process.

Assessment centre A group of activities and tests normally held at an employer's office or in a hotel.

Avatar Online virtual person who can interact with others in the virtual world of an online gaming community or even a chatroom.

BACS An acronym for Bankers Automated Clearing Services; it is the UK scheme for electronic processing of financial transactions.

Blog Short for web log, it is an online diary or article written by anyone who has something to say. Some companies post employee blogs on their website to provide an informal view of the company that may be attractive to prospective job candidates or clients alike.

Chatroom Online group forum for discussion on any given topic. This often takes place in real time, using applications such as instant messaging.

CV uploader Online tool that enables CVs to be transferred from a candidate's computer to a recruiter's website or holding area.

EEA An acronym for European Economic Area, which provides a single market for the free movement of labour and services, as well as most capital and products. It comprises all the members of the European Union and the European Free Trade Association, with the exception of Switzerland.

e-tray exercise A recruitment test that asks you to organise your electronic inbox (your e-tray), delegating, referring up and dealing with tasks against the clock. You will normally be asked to explain the decisions you took during a follow-up session.

Generation Y University-educated first- or second-jobbers born during the 1980s.

Gardening leave Also known as garden leave, this is where an employer can insist you serve your notice period at home (or in the garden), rather than at work.

Headhunter A recruitment consultant or agency that seeks out potential candidates for jobs, including those people who are not actively seeking new positions.

Job board An online listing of job vacancies, often published by newspapers or by dedicated websites such as Monster.

Magic circle A term regularly used to collectively describe London's top five international corporate law firms.

Microsite Mini website linked to its parent site, but specialising in a specific area such as recruitment. Microsites often also have their own web address.

Milkround A careers fair held at a university or college of higher education. The name was coined because, just like a milkman delivers milk to your door, a graduate recruiter delivers jobs to your university.

Netrep Short for internet reputation. If your YouTube presence is of you frolicking drunkenly, your netrep will be that of a drunk.

Passive candidate Someone who is not actively looking for a job but may be receptive to the right opportunity.

P11D An annual document recording any benefits in kind you have been given during the tax year, such as a company car, interest-free loans or private medical insurance.

P45 A record of what you have been paid to date in the tax year, plus a note of the tax you have paid.

P46 A tax form for employees who have lost their P45 and first jobbers, such as students.

Pdf An acronym for Portable Document Format. This is an electronic document or a scan that can contain text or images or both, which must be read with the Adobe Acrobat computer program.

Personal statement A term that can be interchangeably used to refer to the short personal profile normally found on a CV, or the longer supporting statement that is common to many standard application forms.

Podcast Information contained in an audio format that can be played on an MP3 player or through a PC. Some recruiters enable information to be downloaded from their websites via podcasts.

Psychometric test A term that applies to a raft of ability, personality and interest questionnaires or examinations. Ability-style tests measure aptitude, attainment and intelligence. Personality and interest questionnaires do not have right or wrong answers.

Restrictive covenants Contractual obligations preventing you from competing with your current employer after you have left employment with them.

SME Small to medium-sized enterprises, typically numbering 1–250 employees.

Social networking sites Websites such as MySpace, Facebook and Bebo that encourage communication and relationships between online users.

Thread Topic of conversation addressed by group of forum or chatroom users.

Viral advertising Messages or concepts that are compelling enough to make people want to pass them on, often through chatrooms or email messaging.

Useful addresses

Age Concern
Astral House
1268 London Road
London SW16 4ER
Tel: 0800 00 99 66
www.ageconcern.co.uk

The Age and Employment Network
207–221 Pentonville Road
London N1 9UZ
Tel: 020 7843 1590
www.taen.org.uk

Age Positive
Helpline: 0113 232 4444
www.agepositive.gov.uk
(Part of the Department of Work and
Pensions, supporting older people into
employment)

Careers Northern Ireland
Tel: 028 9044 1781
www.careersserviceni.com

Careers Scotland
Tel: 0845 850 2502
www.careers-scotland.org.uk

Careers Wales
Tel: 0800 100 900
www.careerswales.com or
www.gyrfacymru.com

Chartered Institute of Personnel and Development (CIPD)
151 The Broadway
London SW19 1JQ
Tel: 020 8612 6200
www.cipd.co.uk

ChildcareLink
Tel: 08000 96 02 96
www.childcarelink.gov.uk
(Government-funded strategy to help people
back into the workplace by removing the
childcare barrier)

Citizens Advice Bureau (CAB)
Check telephone directory for local office
www.adviceguide.org.uk

Commission for Equality and Human Rights (CEHR)
3 More London
Riverside
Tooley Street
London SE1 2RG
Tel: 0800 0181 259
www.equalityhumanrights.com
(Founded on 1 October 2007, The
Commission for Equality and Human Rights
took over the roles of the former
Commission for Racial Equality, the Disability
Rights Commission and the Equal
Opportunities Commission)

Companies House
Crown Way
Maindy
Cardiff CF14 3UZ
Tel: 0870 33 33 636
www.companieshouse.gov.uk

Connexions Direct (England)
Tel: 080 800 13219
www.connexions-direct.com
(Careers advice)

Employment Opportunities for People
with Disabilities
53 New Broad Street
London EC2M 1SL
Tel: 020 7448 5420
www.opportunities.org.uk

Gangmaster Licensing Authority (GLA)
PO Box 8538
Nottingham
NG8 9AF
Tel: 0845 602 5020
www.gla.gov.uk

HM Revenue & Customs (HMRC)
www.hmrc.gov.uk
For your local tax office, check your
telephone directory or see
www.hmrc.gov.uk/local/individuals/

Home Office's Border & Immigration
Agency
Lunar House
40 Wellesley Road
Croydon
CR9 2BY
Tel: 0870 606 7766
www.workingintheuk.gov.uk

Jobcentre Plus
Tel: 0845 606 0234
Textphone: 0800 023 4888
www.jobcentreplus.gov.uk

Jobseeker Direct
Tel: 0845 6060 234
Textphone: 0845 6055 255

The Knowledge Transfer Partnership
Momenta
Didcot
Oxfordshire OX11 0QJ
Tel: 0870 190 2829
www.ktponline.org.uk

Learndirect
Tel: 0800 100 900 (8am–10pm daily)
www.learndirect-advice.co.uk

Learning and Skills Council
Cheylesmore House
Quinton Road
Coventry CV1 2WT
Tel: 0845 019 4170
Help desk: 0870 900 6800
www.lsc.gov.uk
For modern apprenticeships, see
www.apprenticeships.org.uk

Mind
15–19 Broadway
London E15 4BQ
Tel: 0845 766 0163 (9.15am–5.15pm,
Mon–Fri)
www.mind.org.uk
(Mental healthy charity with information on
employment, education and training
opportunities for people with mental illnesses)

National Association for the Care and
Resettlement of Offenders (NACRO)
169 Clapham Road
London SW9 0PU
Tel: 0800 0181 259
Helpline: 0800 0181 259
www.nacro.org.uk

National Council for Voluntary Service
177 Arundel Street
Sheffield S1 2NU
Tel: 0114 278 6636
www.nacvs.org.uk

Prison Advice and Care Trust (PACT)
Suite C5 City Cloisters
196 Old Street
London EC1V 9FR
Tel: 020 7490 3139
www.prisonadvice.org.uk

REACH (England)
89 Albert Embankment
London SE1 7TP
Tel: 020 7582 6543
www.reach-online.org.uk
(Matches the skills of experienced people to
the needs of voluntary organisations)

**Recruitment and Employment
Confederation**
36–38 Mortimer Street
London W1W 7RG
Tel: 020 7462 3260
www.rec.uk.com

Remploy
Stonecourt
Siskin Drive
Coventry CV3 4FJ
Tel: 0800 138 7656
www.remploy.co.uk
(Finds employment opportunities for people
with disabilities)

Rethink
28 Castle Street
Kingston upon Thames
Surrey KT1 1SS
Tel: 020 8974 6814 (10am–3pm, Mon–Fri)
www.rethink.org
(Charity provider of mental health services)

RNID
19–23 Featherstone Street
London EC1Y 8SL
Tel: 020 7296 8000
www.rnid.org.uk
(Support and advice for people with hearing
impairments)

Shaw Trust
Fox Talbot House
Greenways Business Park
Malmesbury Road
Chippenham
Wiltshire SN15 1BN

Tel: 01225 716 350
www.shaw-trust.org.uk
(Provides support, training and supported
employment projects for people with
disabilities or ill health)

Shell Step
Step Enterprise Ltd
14 Bridgford Rd
West Bridgford
Nottingham NG2 6AB
Tel: 0870 036 5450
www.step.org.uk
(UK-wide programme providing work
experience for undergraduates)

Social Firms UK
1st Floor, Furness House
53 Brighton Road
Redhill
Surrey RH1 6PZ
Tel: 01737 764 021
www.socialfirms.co.uk
(Creates employment opportunities for
disabled people through the development
and support of social firms)

Surestart
Sure Start Unit
Department for Education and Skills and
Department for Work and Pensions
Level 2, Caxton House
Tothill Street
London SW1H 9NA
Tel: 0870 000 2288
www.surestart.gov.uk

Timebank
3 Downstream Building
1 London Bridge
London SE1 9BG
Tel: 0845 456 1668
www.timebank.org.uk
(Connecting volunteers with work
opportunities)

213

Tomorrow's People
4th Floor, Rothermere House
49–51 Cambridge Road
Hastings
East Sussex TN34 1DT
Tel: 01424 718491
www.tomorrows-people.org.uk
(Helping people with disadvantages find work)

Training and Development Agency for Schools
Portland House
Stag Place
London SW1E 5TT
Tel: 0870 4960 123
www.teach.gov.uk

Voluntary Service Overseas (VSO)
317 Putney Bridge Road
London SW15 2PN
Tel: 020 8780 7200
www.vso.org.uk

Volunteering England
Regents Wharf
8 All Saints Street
London N1 9RL
Tel: 0845 305 6979
www.volunteering.org.uk

Working Families
1–3 Berry Street
London EC1V 0AA
Tel: 020 7253 7243
www.workingfamilies.org.uk
(Offers free information and advice to parents on employment and childcare issues)

CAREERS ADVICE AND JOB BOARDS FOR GRADUATES
www.get.hobsons.co.uk
www.milkround.com
www.prospects.ac.uk

CAREERS ADVICE FOR PEOPLE RETURNING TO OR LEAVING WORK
www.changingdirection.com
www.iambeingfired.co.uk
www.i-resign.com/uk
www.motheratwork.co.uk

JOB BOARDS
wwwfish4jobs.co.uk
www.guardianjobs.co.uk
www.jobserve.co.uk
www.localgovernmentchannel.com
www.monster.co.uk
www.totaljobs.com

RECRUITMENT AGENCIES & HEADHUNTERS
Archibald and Dutch
www.archibald-and-dutch.com
Bluefire Consulting
www.bluefireconsulting.co.uk
Brook Street
www.brookstreet.co.uk
Chase International
www.chaseman.co.uk
Graduate Recruitment Bureau
www.grb.uk.com
ITN Mark Education
www.markeducation.co.uk
Manpower
www.manpower.co.uk
Michael Page
www.michaelpage.co.uk
Office Angels
www.officea-angels.com
Persona
www.persona.eu.com
Reed
www.reed.co.uk
Robert Walters
www.robertwalters.com
Rockall Recruitment
www.rockall.co.uk
Twinserve
www.twinserve.com

Index

which?

Which? is the leading independent consumer champion in the UK.
A not-for-profit organisation, we exist to make individuals as powerful as the organisations they deal with in everyday life. The next few pages give you a taster of our many products and services. For more information, log onto www.which.co.uk or call 0800 252 100.

Which? Online

www.which.co.uk gives you access to all Which? content online and much, much more. It's updated regularly, so you can read hundreds of product reports and Best Buy recommendations, keep up to date with Which? campaigns, compare products, use our financial planning tools and interactive car-buying guide. You can also access all the reviews from *The Which? Good Food Guide*, ask an expert in our interactive forums, register for e-mail updates and browse our online shop – so what are you waiting for? To subscribe, go to www.which.co.uk.

Which? Legal Service

Which? Legal Service offers immediate access to first-class legal advice at unrivalled value. One low-cost annual subscription allows members to enjoy unlimited legal advice by telephone on a wide variety of legal topics, including consumer law – problems with goods and services, employment law, holiday problems, neighbour disputes, parking, speeding and clamping fines and probate administration. To subscribe, call the membership hotline: 0800 252 100 or go to www.whichlegalservice.co.uk.

Which? Computing

If you own a computer, are thinking of buying one or just want to keep abreast of the latest technology and keep up with your kids, there's one invaluable source of information you can turn to – *Which? Computing* magazine. *Which? Computing* offers you honest unbiased reviews of the best (and worst) new technology, problem-solving tips from the experts and step-by-step guides to help you make the most of your computer. To subscribe, go to www.computingwhich.co.uk.

Which? Books

which?

Which? Books

Other books in this series

Buy, Sell and Move House

Kate Faulkner
ISBN: 978 1 84490 043 5
Price £10.99

Featuring the 2007 government changes to HIPs legislation. A complete, no-nonsense guide to negotiating the property maze and making your move as painless as possible. From dealing with estate agents to chasing solicitors and working out the true cost of your move, this guide tells you how to keep things on track and avoid painful sticking points.

Develop your Property

Kate Faulkner
ISBN: 978 1 84490 038 1
Price £10.99

Develop your Property is aimed at the thousands of people in the UK who are looking to make a serious and long-term investment in their property. Covering planning permission and building regulations, this guide deals with property development in a jargon-free and unbiased manner.

Renting and Letting

Kate Faulkner
ISBN: 978 1 84490 029 9
Price £10.99

A practical guide for landlords, tenants, and anybody considering the buy-to-let market. Written by a practicing property professional, this real-world guide covers all the legal and financial matters, including tax, record-keeping and mortgages, as well as disputes, deposits and security.

Which? Books

Which? Books provide impartial, expert advice on everyday matters from finance to law, property to major life events. We also publish the country's most trusted restaurant guide, *The Which? Good Food Guide*. To find out more about Which? Books, log on to www.which.co.uk or call 01903 828557.

" Which? tackles the issues that really matter to consumers and gives you the advice and active support you need to buy the right products. **"**